BRITISH POLICY AND

THE NATIONALIST MOVEMENT IN BURMA

ASIAN STUDIES AT HAWAII

The Publications Committee of the Asian Studies
Program will consider all manuscripts for inclusion
in the series, but primary consideration will be
given to the research results of graduate students
and faculty at the University of Hawaii. The
series includes monographs, occasional papers,
translations with commentaries, and research aids.

Orders for Asian Studies at Hawaii publications
should be directed to The University Press of
Hawaii, 535 Ward Avenue, Honolulu, Hawaii 96814.
Present standing orders will continue to be filled
without special notification.

Asian Studies at Hawaii, No. 11

BRITISH POLICY AND

THE NATIONALIST MOVEMENT IN BURMA

1917-1937

Albert D. Moscotti

Asian Studies Program
University of Hawaii

The University Press of Hawaii

1974

The Asian Studies Program of the University of
Hawaii offers multidisciplinary course work leading
to the bachelor's and master's degrees in East
Asian, Southeast Asian, and South Asian Studies.
In addition, it encourages research and scholarly
projects related to Asia. Many departments of
the University of Hawaii award advanced degrees
for studies dealing with Asia.

Library of Congress Catalog Card Number 73-86163

ISBN 0-8248-0279-9

TABLE OF CONTENTS

FOREWORD

Many years ago, while using the Yale University Library collection on Burma, I discovered this study as others had before me. After reading it, I wondered why it had not been published. My curiosity grew as I found references to it and quotations from it in other publications. When I first met Moscotti in 1967, I found the answer without asking. As a Foreign Service Officer he had little or no time to devote to private scholarly matters. Only now, having retired from the Foreign Service and having begun a new career in education has he, at last, found time to make minor changes in the text and notes and see the manuscript through publication.

Why publish this study now? Surely, in the more than twenty years since it was written, new studies have been produced which reflect new data, methodology, and the availability of documents and memoirs not accessible when Moscotti was writing. I give three important reasons in answer to this question. First, it is a solid piece of scholarship written in a dispassionate and objective manner. It has helped a generation of interested readers understand the complex developments in

Burma and, as noted earlier, has been referred to and quoted in publications by some of the leading scholars on Burma. On the basis of its place in the literature, this study should be made available to as wide an audience as possible so that new readers can profit by it as I and others did over the past two decades.

Second, there has not been sufficient interest in and therefore study of the colonial system and its impact on the land and people of Burma. Recently, Burmese and foreign scholars alike have produced several specialized monographs on the rice trade of Burma, transportation, labor, money, and other topics that grew out of the colonial system. They give partial glimpses of Burma under foreign rule, but do not try to fit the parts together. Many postwar historians have concentrated upon indigenous history in the modern period as a reaction to earlier scholars' concern for colonial administration, law, and economic growth. Others have devoted themselves to a study of pre-Western history in Burma. With the exception of John F. Cady's History of Modern Burma (1958), which surveys the period covered by Moscotti as part of the longer course of Burmese history, there have been no major publications by social scientists since John L. Christian wrote Modern Burma in 1942 and J. S.

viii

Furnivall wrote _Colonial_ _Policy_ _and_ _Practice_ in
1948. Moscotti's study is an important addition
to the literature and will be useful to scholars
for some time to come as they try to understand
colonial policy and its reaction both in broad as
well as in narrow focus.

A third reason for publishing this study is
the current interest among scholars and laymen in
the phenomenon of colonialism. The writings of
Marx and Freud have influenced the writings of
Fanon and Manoni in their search to explain the
causes of colonialism and its psychological effects
upon the ruler and the ruled. Generalizations
about the system do not always correspond with the
reality of a particular form of colonial rule.
Burma like its near neighbor India and its further neighbors Vietnam, Indonesia, and the Philippines were all subjected to various forms of foreign rule. While there were certain similarities--
alien rule, economic exploitation, little or no
modernization and development--each was different.
It is vital to study the particular system better
to understand the impact of colonialism as it
really was and not as it was supposed to have been.
Moscotti's study gives the reader a detailed picture of colonialism in action. His analysis of the
changes and their impact will prove useful to stu-

dents of Burma's history as well as those interested in comparative colonialism. It will force
those who seek easy generalizations to examine the
subject more intensively and deeply.

Finally, I am glad to see this work published,
and I hope that more scholars will be attracted to
the study of its major themes and Burma in general.
Despite Burma's present policy to keep itself
closed to foreign scholars and tourists alike, that
will change. When that time comes we will benefit
from having had studies such as this one to help us
understand Burma's complex past.

Josef Silverstein

Rutgers University
January 22, 1973

x

"British Policy in Burma, 1917-1937," the
original title of this work, was written in 1949-
1950 and accepted as my doctoral dissertation at
Yale University in 1950. My interest in Burma and
Southeast Asia originally stemmed from service in
northern Burma with the U.S. Army Air Corps during
World War II. This interest was further stimulated
by some of the distinguished Southeast Asia specialists on the Yale faculty at that time--John
Embree, Raymond Kennedy, Paul Mus, and Karl Pelzer,
among others. Professor Arnold Wolfers encouraged
me to write my dissertation on Burma.

I joined the Department of State in 1949 and
eventually the U.S. Foreign Service, serving in
Bangkok, Karachi, Madras, and Kuala Lumpur as well
as in Washington. A trip through the Mergui Archi-
pelago from Phuket, Thailand to Rangoon on a coastal
steamer in the mid-1950s, capped by a brief visit
to Mandalay, heightened my interest in Burma. It
was not until I retired from the Foreign Service
and joined the faculty at the University of Hawaii
in 1970 that I was able to take up my dissertation
on Burma again.

Several specialists on Burma and Southeast

Asia have encouraged me to have the dissertation published. I have no illusions that this is the definitive work on the period, especially since no Burmese language sources were used, nor does this work advance any startling, new interpretations of events. But this work was something of a pioneer effort and did offer a real service, I believe, by providing a thorough inventory and study of English-language primary sources on political developments relating to Burma (1917-1937), available in the United States at that time. Also, I believe, this work provides a balanced account of major events relating to political development in Burma from 1917 to 1937 and reasonable assessments of their significance. The fact that a number of leading authorities on Burma, who have published since 1950, have cited my dissertation strengthens these convictions.

I have not attempted a complete revision. I have carefully studied major secondary works covering my subject that have appeared since my dissertation was completed. (The most notable work in this regard is John F. Cady's A History of Modern Burma.) I then reexamined my manuscript in the light of these secondary works and, in cases which they provide important new evidence or convincing new interpretations of events, I have made

xii

brief additions to or modifications of my text.
None of these secondary works indicated to me that
major revisions of my dissertation were required.
The title was changed to: British Policy and the
Nationalist Movement in Burma, 1917-1937.

My indebtedness to John S. Furnivall is apparent to anyone familiar with his perceptive first-
hand observations and analysis of Burma's recent
history. Furnivall's assessment of the impact
of British rule on the political, economic, and
social institutions of Burma was especially valuable, particularly in helping to devise the framework of analysis for parts of this work. Everyone
concerned with the study of modern Burma and with
the analysis of colonial regimes owes much to the
great contributions made by Furnivall.

I am indebted to Cecil Hobbs, formerly "Mr.
Southeast Asia" at the Library of Congress, for
his patient and expert assistance in uncovering
materials on Burma. A special vote of thanks is
extended to Professor Josef Silverstein, Rutgers
University, for his encouragement in the publication of this book, for reading the revised manuscript, and for kindly writing a foreword. I am
responsible, of course, for all factual data,
analysis, and interpretation. Finally, I am most
grateful to Mrs. Sharon Ishida, Overseas Career

Program, University of Hawaii, for preparing the
typed manuscript.

Albert D. Moscotti

SPECIAL NOTE

In this study, the noun "Burmese," employed
in the 1953 Census of the Union of Burma, is used
for the major ethnic group in the country. The
term "Burman" is used for this ethnic group in
some other studies and was also used by officials in
Burma and India during the British regime. Either
form appears acceptable. (See Frank M. Lebar,
Gerald C. Hickey, and John K. Musgrave, Ethic
Groups of Mainland Southeast Asia /New Haven:
Human Relations Area Files Press, 1964/, p. 30.)

In some parts of this work, the Burmese are
referred to exclusively, even though other indigenous peoples of Burma might also have been involved
in or affected by the developments under discussion.
This practice has been followed because one of the
main foci of this study is the interaction between
the British administration and the nationalist
movement which essentially was Burmese.

CHAPTER 1

BRITISH POLICY IN BURMA PRIOR TO 1917

On January 4, 1948, the new flag of the independent
Union of Burma was unfurled in Rangoon marking the
end of over a hundred years of the British rule in
Burma. The leaders of Burma assumed the responsibility for governing their country and promoting
the welfare of their people. [The Burmese had acquired most of their limited experience with modern
political institutions under the special conditions
of colonialism.[1]] Indeed, preparation for political
self-rule had been a fundamental component of
governmental policy in Burma as the British administration faced the challenge of Burmese
nationalism in the period between the two world
wars. The efficacy of the British program of
political tutelage and the effectiveness of the
Burmese leadership which developed during the
period between World War I and World War II have
proved to be significant factors in determining
the future of Burma as a sovereign state.

The British conquest of the kingdom of Burma
had been accomplished in three stages during the
nineteenth century.[2] The segments of Burma had

been appended to the Indian Empire, finally being consolidated as a province. Burma remained an Indian province until 1937, when it became a separate British colony. More than two-thirds of the 13 million inhabitants of Burma were engaged in agriculture, chiefly rice cultivation. The indigenous population was overwhelmingly Buddhist and culturally closer to the Thai than to the Indians to whom they were joined politically. Monastery schools provided a high male literacy rate (30 percent) compared with other Asian peoples. Once the British administration secured its hold on Burma, the population tended to accept British rule and was regarded as politically apathetic.

The political resurrection of Burma was activated by the decision of the British government in 1917 to promote "the gradual development of self-governing institutions" in India.[3] Since the conquest of Burma, the focus of British policy had centered on the establishment and maintenance of conditions conducive to economic expansion in this new province of India, almost to the exclusion of political growth. The political reforms which were introduced between 1917 and 1935 were circumscribed by "safeguards" that would reasonably assure conditions conducive to economic growth and permit the ultimate power of decision making to remain in the

2

hands of the British administrator. Within these limitations, significant advances were made in "the progressive realization of responsible government" in Burma between the policy statement of 1917 and 1937 when the second major constitutional reform was placed in operation.

British policy in Burma gradually lost its laissez faire tendencies with the completion of the annexation in 1886 and the intensification of economic activity in the newly won colony. [From the first, the immediate concerns of the British administrators in Burma were efficient administration and the maintenance of law and order.] This became a progressively more difficult task with the gradual disintegration of the indigenous social structure which followed the encroachment of Western economic and political institutions.[4] [The administrative patterns were usually transported from India to British Burma without sufficient adaptation to local conditions.] The system of direct administration through British officials down to the district level was instituted in Burma. In this attempt to make the government both rational and efficient, a system of "gradationary control" was devised whereby authority would be exercised and responsibility exacted through a clearly defined chain of officials on a territorial basis. Though this system recognized the fundamental importance of the local community in administration, it was contrary to the Burmese village system in which authority was personal and, in some cases, loosely hereditary. While the traditional social controls on the village level lost their hold with the deterioration of customary local rule, the system of direct administration and impersonal law failed to fill the void created in the Burmese society. This basic maladjustment spawned consequences prejudicial to the welfare of the peasant and the interest of the Burma government and frustrated many of the policies aimed at the development of self-governing institutions.[5]

The impact of British institutions on the people of Burma was demonstrated by the operation of the new tax structure, the legal system, and the economic policies accompanying British rule. In fiscal administration the British replaced a variety of Burmese taxes in kind by new taxes designed to raise the revenue necessary for the functioning of a modern government.[6]

Nineteenth-century Western liberalism with its tenets of equality before the law, free trade, and individual rights provided the basis of the political and economic philosophies that shaped the character of British rule in Burma. Restrictions on commerce, which had hampered trade under Burmese rule, were swept away. Teak licenses were granted on generous terms to British firms. The government went so far as to encourage immigration of Indian labor by paying a per capita bounty. In general, however, laissez faire policies prevailed. The function of the administration was to maintain law and order and a sound financial position.

The introduction of Western jurisprudence replaced the existing Burmese controls based on personal authority by a system of impersonal law. The new juridical order, consistent with the British legal experience and based on the concepts of liberalism, was essential to the development of economic enterprises depending on contract enforcement. This legal transformation was thus closely associated with the other objectives of British policy in Lower Burma. Even in this earlier period, however, laissez faire was being naturally replaced by more positive policies aimed at promoting a climate conducive to the economic growth of British interests in Burma.

The earlier British entrepreneurs in Burma were involved almost solely in the commerce of teak and rice. It was the government that laid the first railroad in Lower Burma in 1874 and equipped the river transportation system.[7] The annexation

of Upper Burma in 1886 was followed by new direct
investments of British capital in rice mills, mines,
oil wells, and, on a smaller scale, in rubber plan-
tations. With the exceptions noted, the British
government in Burma did not actively interest
itself in public services and welfare until about
the turn of the century. The emphasis on public
order, economic liberalism, and efficient administration persisted. Nevertheless positive steps
were taken in promoting economic development under
the government's public works program. Military
considerations were important in the sporadic
efforts at road building which took place prior
to the final conquest of Burma. Limited by a lack
of funds and personnel, government engineers
erected river embankments in the delta region,
developed the irrigation system of Upper Burma and
established the rudiments of a communications system. This public works program, inadequate and
tailored to meet special needs rather than the
broad public interests, signalized the beginnings
of more active government participation in the
economic development of Burma.[8]

In keeping with the policy of administrative
efficiency, the coastal provinces gained in 1826
and 1852 were consolidated as British Burma in
1862. Administrative machinery, following the

6

Indian prototype, was reorganized along functional lines in key fields such as police, revenue, and, to a rudimentary degree, health services. Despite this increasing complexity of the structure of the British government in Burma, the administrative policy remained essentially one of laissez faire.

In an effort to regularize administration and fix responsibility for revenue collection and law and order, the British overhauled the system of local government. Earlier attempts to impose direct rule had been only partially successful, but the pacification of Burma following the conquest of 1886 made possible the implementation of mechanistic plans for village rule. Many of the traditional powers of local Burmese leaders were withdrawn or reassigned, often without adequate regard for their organic derivation, and were made subject to close regulation from above. The units of administration were fragmented in conformity with a preconceived pattern imported from India.

The effectiveness of the revised system of village administration as an agency for the preservation of law and order and the collection of revenues was the chief criterion by which the new system of local government was evaluated. Some of the experienced British officials fully appreciated the importance of the Burmese social institutions, but there was little real understanding of the functioning of the indigenous society and its relation to British rule. In order to standardize the scheme of local government the Burmese leaders were made petty officials and their functions were differentiated to establish lines of responsibility. For administrative convenience, decentralization was effected so that there would be one village for one _thugyi_ (headman). This was consistent with the introduction of impersonal law down to the village level in place of the traditional personal authority of the circle headman over several villages. Under British rule the village community relationships in rural Burma were disrupted, the Burmese local official dissociated from the populace, and the individual released from the restraints of custom and tradition. The administrative system introduced by the British, devoted to economic development and efficiency, failed to fill the gap it created by displacing the Burmese regime. The progressive social disintegration that ensued, coupled with associated agrarian problems, generated an environment which impaired the development of self-governing institutions.[9]

The British administration, though interested from the first in the economic development of Burma by British traders and entrepreneurs, confined

8

itself initially to such activities as removing
old Burmese trade restrictions, granting licenses
for the exploitation of natural resources, and
encouraging labor immigration. Gradually, through
a limited public works program, the growth of
functional services and the inclusion of representatives of economic interests in the Governor's Council, the British policy in Burma abandoned laissez
faire and provided for government participation in
economic development. The most significant political reform in the Burma government in the pre-1917
period was the constitution of the Legislative
Council in 1897. This advisory group, subsequently
enlarged, reflected the interests of the increasingly important British economic groups in Burma.[10]

As early as 1856 the government began to give
attention to controlling some aspects of the exploitation of Burma's resources. A Forestry Department was established at that time to carry out con-
servation measures and insure the government revenues from teak concessions.[11] Through licensing
and subsidies, attempts were made to prevent the
most shortsighted economic exploitation.[12]

Certain basic public services accompanied
the growth of the government functions related to
economic development. The need for minor officials
and clerks to man the spreading administrative

9

system was responsible in part for the establishment of the Department of Public Instruction in 1866. The schools were operated by either Buddhist monks or foreign missionaries until 1871 when lay schools were established.[13] To provide the basic services needed by towns and cities, municipal councils were constituted in 1874.[14] Administrative organs were devised to deal with health and sanitation. This limited public welfare program was fragmentary, disjointed, and erratic in its operation.[15]

The previous policies and practices of the British administration had established the environment in which political reform had to function. Prior to World War I, political institutions had been created and operated with a view to administrative efficiency and convenience almost to the exclusion of other values. The limited amount of decentralization inaugurated by the Indian government, and then in turn by the Burma government, was essentially a matter of administrative expediency.[16] The 1897 Legislative Council was a convenient mechanism both for administrative decentralization and for giving economic interests a direct voice in the government. This advisory body of nominated members and officials was not devised as an embryo legislature foreshadowing self-rule. In local government the village system innovated by

10

the British replaced Burmese customary local rule
with a rational, nonorganic system which was in
accord with the needs of Western political and
economic institutions. The municipal councils were
narrow in scope and function and lacked a real basis
in the Burmese community. Under British rule
political development in terms of self-governing
institutions received no attention until 1917.

In 1917 the British administrators could point
to increased population, trade, and revenue receipts
as indications of the benefits of policies directed
toward promoting Burma's economic development.
Increments in Burma's national income, however, bore
little relation to the welfare of the individual
peasant.[17] Paralleling the increases in economic
production in Burma was an alarmingly mounting
incidence of crime. Improved police methods were
introduced by the government in an attempt to meet
the increase in murder, dacoity (brigandage), and
other serious crimes, but this approach was inadequate and the uptrend in crime persisted. The
Crime Enquiry Committee, 1923, concluded that the
roots of the problem of lawlessness lay in the
conditions of the peasants, although the committee
failed to go far enough in searching out the sources
of these conditions.[18] The growth of crime was
directly related to the deterioration of the Burmese

11

social structure, which had provided the traditional restraints on antisocial behavior. This breakdown in rural society was in turn a by-product of the rapid expansion of commercialized agriculture fostered by a government primarily interested in economic development and efficient administration. The customary pattern of life in Burma, geared to a subsistence economy under a system of personal rule and authority, was disrupted by the new colonial system and rapidly lost its cohesiveness. These conditions created an environment in which attempts to foster the growth of self-rule would necessarily face serious obstacles.

The adverse repercussions of early British policies were most severe in the rural districts and villages, and consequently the administrators on the operational level experienced extreme difficulties in implementing later policies directed toward the spread of self-governing institutions. Turbulent conditions prevailed for five years after the annexation of Upper Burma in 1886 that prevented the stabilization of society on established lines.[19] Most of the British officials sent to Burma had previously served as civil servants in India. This prior experience, coupled with the predilection of the central government in India for established political forms, increased the propensity to trans-

12

fer political institutions and administrative practices bodily from India to Burma without adequate adaptation to the peculiar conditions in Burma.[20] Another major difficulty in implementing British policy was the inadequacy and inaccuracy of the information on which the British policy makers based their administration, particularly with regard to the character of Burmese society.[21]

[The absence of a long-range program to check the spread of absentee landlordism and rural indebtedness, which followed the commercialization of rice cultivation, was the most significant gap in the economic controls devised by the British administrators.] The commercialization of rice cultivation by opening new paddy lands in the undeveloped lower Irrawaddy Valley required labor and capital. Initially these two factors were provided by Burmese migrating from Upper Burma. Soon Indian immigrants were utilized to provide seasonal labor at a low wage while Indian money lenders became the principal source of capital. Concomitant with increasing rice exports were growing absentee landlordism, tenant farming, and agricultural indebtedness.[22] The Land Improvement Loan Act (1883) and the Agricultural Loan Act (1884) were perfunctory and ineffectual measures aimed at improving the conditions of the peasants. The mounting agrarian problems of the peasants of Burma contributed to the disintegration which attended the reorganization of the village system to produce an unstable social order. The failure of the British administration to take hold of these fundamental problems was an underlying cause of conditions which impeded the political development of Burma.

The presence of economically important non-indigenous minorities in Burma complicated the constitutional problem with regard to the development of self-governing institutions and affected Burmese nationalism. Indian laborers, artisans, merchants, and money lenders were the most numerous of these minorities and, next to the British, the most significant politically.

In 1917 Burma, the largest province of India, had been completely under British sovereignty only thirty years. In that short time considerable growth had occurred in trade, communications, population, and in cultivated acreage. The Governor-General in New Delhi who, was responsible to Parliament in London for the government of Burma, established general policies for the province. Differences of opinion between Rangoon and New Delhi, particularly over revenues and political reforms, persisted until Burma was separated from India in 1937.

14

The Burmese and other indigenous peoples of
Burma were confined almost exclusively to the subordinate and provincial civil services, which
filled the minor positions. The Indian Civil
Service was made up of British and Indian administrators who held the more important posts. Through
these officials, the executive arm administered the
affairs of Burma with the assistance of a Legislative Council that was restricted in scope and
powers.

Villages were nominally ruled by a thugyi
appointed by the deputy commissioner for the area.
These thugyi were responsible for village welfare,
but their chief functions were maintaining public
order and collecting revenues.

In 1917 the Burmese faced a period of accelerating political change with little comprehension,
and almost no experience with modern institutions
of self-government. The ostensible economic well-
being and political contentment of the people of
Burma were almost imperceptibly being undermined
by mounting agrarian problems and social disintegration. Burma was administered by a competent
group of civil servants who were skeptical of
political reform and yet were charged with the task
of implementation of the 1917 policy. The obstacles
which the development of self-government faced were

manifold, and it would require patience, under-

standing, and accommodation on all sides to transfer

successfully political power to the people of Burma.

CHAPTER 2

THE NATIONALIST AWAKENING IN BURMA

Burma, politically dormant for nearly twenty-five
years, was caught up in the Indian reform movement
in 1917. There developed an increasingly insistent
nationalist movement which demanded greater participation in the government and in the benefits of
the economy. Modern Burmese nationalism developed
into a dynamic and often incalculable consideration
for British policy makers

The forces that contributed to this emerging
national consciousness were discernible prior to
the period of political ferment, which developed
after 1917. The Burmese, comprising about
three-quarters of the country's population, were
a homogeneous people with a common store of traditions, customs, and experiences.[1] The older genera-
tions could still recall the reign of the Burmese
kings when Burma was an independent monarchy. The
British military forces had required five years to
pacify Burma after they had deposed King Thibaw in
1886, though there had been no significant opposition to British rule after the pacification was
completed. Burma became a province of the Indian

Empire and, as a result, the special interests of
Burma were subordinated to the broader considerations of Empire policy.

The Burmese peasant only slowly became aware of
the world beyond his own geographically isolated
land. The Burmese kings had been addressed as "the
Overlord of all Kings of the Orient," and vestiges
of this Burmese ethnocentrism persisted into the
twentieth century. National awareness, coupled
with a distrust of foreigners, did not become a
well-articulated nationalist movement until it came
in contact with Western political ideologies and
institutions. The adaptation of Western ideologies
and institutions to the aspirations and demands of
a homogeneous society produced the matrix from
which the Burmese nationalist movement developed.
Through a process of political acculturation the
emerging leaders of Burma acquired the ideas,
symbols, and political formulae which were to
characterize the nationalist movement.[2] The impact
of these new ideas was heightened by the emphasis
on concepts of democracy and self-determination
which accompanied World War I. The Burmese who
encountered Western ideas and came into contact
with the British elite became increasingly aware of
the dynamics and the potential for social change
in the heretofore static Burmese society.[3]

18

The experiences of other Asian peoples were still another influence in the growth of the nationalist movement in Burma. Western political concepts had already been seized upon by other Asian nations and had found expression in the Indian _swaraj_ (self-rule) movement, the revolutionary doctrines of Sun Yat-sen in China, and in the rise of Japan to the status of a major power. The victory of an Asian power over an European state, as in the Russo-Japanese War, had a decided impact on politically conscious elements in Asia, although the interchange of ideas and experiences was very limited.[4] Japan, a Buddhist nation, did attract the attention of some early Burmese leaders. As early as 1910, U Ottama, a Burmese _pongyi_, or monk, who became the spiritual leader of the nationalist movement, visited Japan. An account of the Russo-Japanese War was published in Burma at the beginning of World War I.[5]

The independence of the neighboring Buddhist kingdom of Siam reminded the Burmese of their former sovereign status. Yet the British administration firmly maintained that the Burmese were not yet capable of self-rule.[6]

The most significant political influences on Burmese nationalism in terms of breaking the trail on the pathway to greater self-government projected

19

from India. [If Burma had been politically isolated from India, its progress toward self-rule
would have been slower and more uncertain.] The
Indian nationalists generally set the pace for
reform and demonstrated methods of political
action. [The boycott, the hartal (cessation
of commerce), and the legislative walkout were
techniques of political agitation which spread
to Burma from India.] The decision of British
policy makers to separate Burma from India aroused
the suspicions and active opposition of the more
extreme Burmese nationalists, who saw the move as
one to deny the province of Burma the reforms
being granted to the rest of India.

On the other hand, the economic activities
of the Indian money lenders and low wage laborers
and the authority wielded by the Indian officials
employed by the government in Burma generated
animosities between the Burmese and the Indian
minority. Ill feeling toward Indians was a
strong factor in provoking the more vigorous
expressions of Burmese nationalism and in
arousing sentiment for separation from India.
At the same time, Burma's nationalist leaders
insisted that Burma advance politically at the
same pace as India.

Increasing dissatisfaction with social and

20

economic conditions pervaded the nationalist
movement in the post-1917 era. The growing
agrarian distress generated widespread popular
demands for a redress of grievances. The new
leaders in Burma, equipped with Western political
ideas and techniques, espoused these popular
demands. By harnessing the force of agrarian
discontent to the nationalist movement, the
Burmese leaders gained added strength in their
campaigns for self rule.

Although the Buddhist clergy had declined in
authority, and the close association of Buddhism
with the everyday life of the villager had grown
more lax by the twentieth century, the bond of
religion remained the most cohesive force in
Burmese society. The defense of Buddhism against
the nonbeliever was a rallying cry for the emerging
Burmese nationalists.[7] In 1906 the Young Men's
Buddhist Association (YMBA) was formed, and for
about ten years this organization interested itself
in religion, morals, and education. This was the
only widespread public organization in Burma. Its
early leaders were political moderates who were
Western educated. One of the prominent men in the
YMBA, U Kin, later was knighted while another, U
May Oung, became a member of the high court of Burma. By 1916 this organization began to take on

political functions under the initiative of some
of its younger members. In 1918 the YMBA had some
fifty branches in the larger towns. The controversy over the first constitutional reforms lasting
from 1917 until 1923 completed the metamorphosis
of the YMBA from a social group to a political
organization.[8]

The political tranquility in Burma was accepted
as the natural course of events by the British
administration. The Indian revolutionary movement
spilled over into Burma during the first years of
World War I but failed to incite the Burmese. The
sedition committee appointed by the government of
India in 1918 could find no significant conspiracies connected with the Indian revolutionary movement and involving peoples of Burma, despite a
vigorous campaign carried on by the Indian
agitators.[9]

In an apparent effort to arouse support from
the indifferent Burmese during World War I, the
governor of Burma appointed a committee of three
educators, in 1916, to advise on methods "to encourage the growth of the imperial idea and a sense
of personal loyalty to the King-Emperor in schools
and colleges."[10] The Committee on the Imperial
Idea, while recognizing "that there is no lack of
passive loyalty in Burma, /and/ that the Burman of

22

today after years of settled government and material prosperity acquiesces in the Imperial connection," sought means of inspiring active loyalty by associating the welfare of Burma with the well-being of the Empire.[11] In order to achieve this objective, the appendix to the committee's report suggested that schools should inculcate "a sane and enthusiastic national spirit" teaching the student to know and appreciate his homeland. The motto should be "'Burma for the Burmans' within the Empire." Out of patriotism for Burma the government should attempt to develop loyalty to the Empire. "Nationalism must come first."[12]

Despite the British belief that political apathy was characteristic of the Burmese, the first rumblings of the nationalist movement were heard during the early war years. The link between Buddhism and Burmese nationalism and the growth of the nationalist feeling was demonstrated in the pagoda footwear controversy. Buddhist tenets forbade the wearing of shoes in pagoda areas but Europeans had generally ignored this rule with impunity. In 1901 and again in 1912, the European practice had been questioned but with no support from the Burmese. Then in 1916, objections were raised by Burmese leaders who were supported by the YMBA. By 1918 the protests had aroused enough attention to cause the government to effect "a closure on public discussion" in the "interest of public tranquility."[13] Buddhist organizations sent memorials to the government in 1919 asking that the rule against footwear in pagoda areas be enforced. Shortly thereafter four European women who were wearing shoes on a pagoda platform were attacked, apparently by pongyis.[14] The pagoda footwear controversy illustrated the beginning of a trend toward the active pursuit of national values through organized political action accompanied by occasional outbursts of violence that was to characterize much of the nationalist movement in Burma.

The first phase of the nationalist drive for increased participation in the government of Burma was precipitated by His Majesty's Secretary of State for India, Edwin Montagu, in the policy statement of August 20, 1917:

The policy of His Majesty's Government, with which the Government of India are in complete accord, is that of the increasing association of Indians in every branch of the administration, and the gradual development of self-governing institutions, with a view to the progressive realization of responsible government in India as an integral part of the British Empire.[15]

As late as September, 1918, the American consul in
Rangoon observed that the Burmese maintained their
usual political calm, almost to the point of apathy
toward their own affairs.[16] However, the Montagu
Declaration and the consequent Burmese mission to
India had aroused the people of Burma from what
the Governor considered a state of "placid contentment."[17] The movement for political reform in Burma
stemmed from this major policy change instituted   *Why?*
by the British government.[18] The YMBA sent a deputation to Calcutta in December, 1917, to place
Burma's case before Montagu and the Viceroy, Lord
Chelmsford, who were conducting a joint investigation into political reform for India. The chief
concern of these Burmese nationalists was that their
province's interests would be overshadowed by those
of India. They proposed that Burma be separated
from India and the foundation be laid for a democratic government under British tutelage.[19]

The few politically active Burmese assumed
that Burma, as a province of India, would participate in the projected constitutional reforms. The
Montagu-Chelmsford Report of April, 1918, stating
that the problem of Burma's political development
would be set aside for separate consideration in
the future, aroused suspicions that Burma would be
denied any real advance toward self-rule. The

possibility that India would receive political benefits denied to Burma intensified nationalist demands among the Burmese.[20] Numerous "mushroom associations" interested in political reform were organized in various parts of Burma and mass meetings were held to discuss the Montagu-Chelmsford recommendations on Burma.[21]

The schismatic character of Burmese political organizations soon became apparent when the YMBA split over its position on the reform program set forth by Governor Craddock in December, 1918. The dynamic nationalists of the so-called Younger Party demanded inclusion under the more liberal scheme for India proposed by Montagu and Chelmsford aiming at eventual self-government within the British Empire. The Younger Party included many of the coming leaders of the nationalist movement such as U Ba Pe and U Thein Maung. The Older Party was willing to accept the more moderate Craddock plan and quickly disappeared from the political scene.[22]

The Younger Party of the YMBA moved to bring Burma's case directly to the attention of the British Parliament. Any doubts about the political awareness of the emerging Burmese nationalists were dispelled when a three-man deputation from Burma arrived in London on August 8, 1919. The YMBA, the Burma Reform League, and associated organiza-

tions had raised £2000 to sponsor this mission.
The deputation, consisting of U Pu, U Ba Pe, and U
Tun Shein, testified before the Parliamentary Joint
Select Committee on the Government of India Bill
and lobbied for inclusion under the Indian reforms.[23] Mass meetings were held in Burma and
telegrams in support of the deputation from Burma
were sent to the Parliamentary committee to impress
upon the committee that Burma was politically
aroused over the impending exclusion of Burma from
the new India Act. (The major center of protest
was Rangoon, where three mass meetings were led by
U Chit Hlaing, who was to head the noncooperation
movement in the 1920s.[24]

    The Joint Select Committee restricted itself
to stating that Burma should receive a constitution
"analogous" to that granted to India. The Government of India Act was passed by Parliament in
December, 1919, but the question of reforms for
Burma remained the subject of a three-way tug-of-
war between London, Delhi, and Rangoon. A second
Burmese deputation was sent to London in June, 1920,
and this group reiterated the demand that Burma
receive reforms equal to those granted to India.
The members of the deputation and its sympathizers
in London renewed their political activities.
Interviews with members of Parliament and with

India Office officials, the presentation of memoranda and statements in the British press were all
utilized to agitate for constitutional reform for
Burma. The deputation returned to Burma in December, 1920, after the India Office had accepted
substantially the scheme granted to India as a
basis for a new Burmese constitution.

However, the involved process by which the
British government undertook to transform the
policy decision of the India Office into law caused
yet further delays in Burma's constitutional advance. The Burma government warned in March, 1921:

> Political agitation here assuming form
> of demand for complete Home Rule and is be-
> coming more bitter in tone. Delay in
> settling Reforms Scheme has already caused
> mischief and further delay would be inex-
> pedient.[25]

The government of India was concerned that
delays over reforms would completely alienate the
YMBA.[26] The increased tempo of Burmese nationalism is reflected in the reports of the Criminal
Investigation Department, which was responsible
for the surveillance of political activity. In
the report for 1919 the "constantly expanding
political agitation and unrest"[27] is noted. In
1920 "political activities increased enormously."[28]

28

The Burmese nationalists now began to diversify
their techniques in the quest for increased participation in the government. Noncooperation and boycott were utilized to harass the government and
disrupt normal political processes. The noncooperation campaign was launched in October, 1920,
when, as a protest against the delay in granting
constitutional reforms, the YMBA called for a boycott of the elections for members to the Indian
Legislative Assembly and Council of State at
Delhi.[29] Since the franchise for electors for
these offices was so narrow, this election was no
real test of the strength of the boycott appeal by
the YMBA.

A more pervasive and protracted effort at noncooperation grew out of the student boycott of the
newly established Rangoon University beginning on
December 4, 1920. The persistent suspicion of
British motives expressed itself in the belief fostered by the YMBA that the restrictive provisions of
the University Act of 1920, establishing the
university, were an effort by the government to make
higher education more difficult, in order to limit
the number of educated Burmese. A student resolution calling for a boycott of the new institution
was issued. Rangoon and Judson colleges, consti-
tuent elements of the new university, were picketed

29

and boycotted by student groups. Burmese political leaders interested themselves in the students' cause and the boycott of Rangoon University assumed the trappings of a nationalist contest with the government. The dispute over Rangoon University broadened into a demand for "national schools," that is, non-government schools unfettered by British support and control. The university boycott initiated a movement that brought nationalism to a wider section of the population of Burma through strikes at all government schools and the attempted institution, in many parts of Burma of national schools emphasizing Burmese language, literature, and history.[30] A national college, set up as a result of the boycott, soon foundered, and the national school movement dissipated by the end of 1922, although some of the national schools survived. In 1924, national schools which met certain standards were made eligible for grants-in-aid from the government.[31] By this process some national schools were gradually absorbed into the government-approved educational system, but the agitation over these schools had already served as a stimulus to Burmese nationalism.

While the nationalist movement in Burma was burgeoning, the reform scheme for Burma was approaching realization in London. Finally on Octo-

30

ber 7, 1921, a notification was published stating that Burma would be constituted a Governor's province under the Government of India Act of 1919.[32] Before these changes could be effected, however, a special Burma Reform Committee was selected to investigate and to make recommendations on the franchise and the transfer of executive powers to ministers. In November, 1921, the committee began its work in Rangoon under Frederick Whyte of the Indian government.

The YMBA, after breaking with the moribund Older Party in 1918, continued to embrace loosely all active elements in the nationalist movement. The growing divergence of opinion within the YMBA became more apparent during the reforms controversy. The moderate groups supported gradual reforms paralleling that which was begun by the British in India in 1919.[33] The more ambitious nationalists now pressed for "home rule" of the dominion type.[34]

The leader in the agitation for home rule was the pongyi, U Ottama. Returning from India, where he was a left-wing member of the Indian National Congress, Ottama traveled about Burma sounding the call for home rule.[35] The demands of Ottama and other nationalists for a broad constitutional advance were arousing opposition to the more limited impending reforms even before the new scheme was

31

put into operation. Ottama was tried and convicted for sedition in June, 1921, and sentenced to ten months' imprisonment.[36]

The Burmese nationalists considered the confinement of Ottama an offense to their religion as well as an attempt to check their political aspirations. The Executive Committee of the General Council of Burmese Associations (GCBA), the more comprehensive successor to the YMBA, issued a call for a _hartal_, a general business shutdown, as a protest. In August, 1921, further noncooperative action was launched by the GCBA. In October the GCBA resolved to boycott the impending investigation by the Whyte Burma Reforms Committee.[37] The Whyte committee reported that "there can be no doubt that many (Burmese) who would gladly have appeared before us were deterred from doing so by fear of treatment which they might receive at the hands of those of their fellow countrymen who had adopted a policy of non-participation."[38]

The GCBA called for intimidation of those participating in the welcome planned for the Prince of Wales during his visit to Burma in January, 1922. In a strong speech in the Legislative Council, Governor Craddock condemned the small clique which had "captured the political machine" and which was now attempting to make His Highness'

32

visit a failure.

The leaders of the boycott were interned, and fifty of their subordinates were ordered out of the districts through which the prince would pass. The government precautions were adequate--the prince's trip through Burma passed without incident.[39]

The nationalist movement was by this time no longer confined to a few politically conscious Burmese but was evident at the village level. Here Burmese nationalism obtained a wider base in the wunthanu athins (nationalist associations),which by 1924 had appeared in almost every village in the province.[40] Initially at least, some of the British officials welcomed the athins as a means of shaping constructive public opinion and checking the mounting crime rate.[41] The athins became, however, the means of carrying out the boycott policy of the GCBA on the village level, where it could be made most effective by actions directed against local government officials. The non-European officials were most vulnerable since they were dependent upon their fellow villagers for their everyday needs. The criminal action taken in the courts against U Ottama, the agitator for home rule, was deeply resented. The Criminal Investigation Department officer who had reported the allegedly seditious speeches by U Ottama was forced to change the locale

33

of his marriage because of the attitude of his home
villagers. The Burmese magistrate, Maung Po Pe, who
tried and convicted U Ottama, was refused supplies
in the local bazaar. The situation was made more
unpleasant for Po Pe when the YMBA ordered a boycott of his sister's funeral. It was only through
the good offices of one _pongyi_ that the necessary
musicians, grave diggers, and priests were made
available for the funeral.[42] These village _athins_,
expanding their activities, set up "shadow administrations" in some districts. Unofficial "courts"
sat in judgment on those who cooperated with the
government. A local _thugyi_ who had crossed his
village _athin_ experienced difficulty in securing
a midwife for his daughter. The midwife who finally
offered her services was sentenced by the self-
constituted _athin_ court to move fifty bags of sand
for ignoring the decision of the _athin_ leaders.[43]
The boycott movement became so obnoxious to officials and prejudicial to the prestige of the government that an Anti-Boycott Act was passed in 1922,
in the teeth of nationalist opposition in the Legislative Council. The use of pressure or intimidation
or the refusal to conduct normal relations because
of political reasons was prohibited.[44]

A split in the omnibus GCBA occurred in June,
1922, over the question of participation in the

34

elections for the newly constituted organs of government, the Circle Boards, and the reformed Legislative Council. (A group of twenty-one GCBA members, including eight members of the GCBA executive council, advocated active participation in the functions of government as a means of working for political advancement. When this policy was rejected by the GCBA, the dissident group broke with the parent association and formed the Twenty-One, or Nationalist Party. U Pu, the Nationalist Party leader, and his deputy, U Ba Pe, convened a meeting of the new organization in September, 1922. This group of moderates declared for participation in the reformed Burma Legislative Council "and agitation therein, in accordance with the mandates of the General Council of Burmese Associations so long and so far as the speedy attainment of Home Rule is not prejudiced thereby."[45] The most politically active group remaining in the original GCBA was the Hlaing-Pu-Gyaw (HPG) Party named for its three leaders.[46] The HPG Party, persisting in its noncooperation policy, decided to boycott the Legislative Council elections.

Although the HPG Party abstained from the November, 1922, elections and in some places actively conducted a boycott campaign, there is no evidence of actual intimidation of voters. The

Nationalists gained twenty-eight of the seventy-
nine elected seats, giving them a plurality in the
new Legislative Council. Slightly less than 7 percent of the eligible voters cast ballots in the
election, but it is difficult to estimate the relative importance of unfamiliarity with procedures,
indifference, and the boycott in accounting for this
feeble turnout.[47] Whatever the reason, the new
Legislative Council could in no way be said to have
had the politically necessary popular base

The Nationalist Party was the only organized
political group which appeared at the opening session of the reformed legislature in 1923. The
Nationalists opposed a loose parliamentary grouping
of government supporters called the Progressive
Party. This coalition embraced conservative Burmese and the nominated representatives of minorities and special interests.[48] The Nationalist
Party policy in the first Legislative Council was
to cooperate in working the reforms as a means to
achieving self-rule. U Maung Gyee, a Nationalist
leader, served as Minister of Education. On the
whole the Nationalist opposition attempted to function with a minimum of obstructionism. The Nationalist Party was supported by the bulk of the Burmese
intelligensia, but the HPG group, backed by the
ubiquitous _pongyis_, had a wider appeal to the

36

masses of Burma.[49]

The favorite target for the Nationalist members of the Legislative Council, particularly in the first session of the reformed legislature, was the police. (Nationalist hostility toward the police arose not only because of the political controls exercised by the police but also because the responsibility for public order rested with the Governor's Executive Councilor and had not been made a transferred subject under the reforms.) The police budget was cut by a vote of 40-37 in March, 1923. When the government's request for a supplementary grant for the police budget was rejected the Governor "certified" the allotment of additional funds by exercising his special powers.[50] Government-sponsored bills all cleared the first reformed Legislative Council (1923-1925), usually without being taken to parliamentary divisions. Nationalist resolutions to release political prisoners, to appoint a crime investigation committee, and to abolish the capitation tax were accepted in toto, or with amendments, by the government. Only eight resolutions were forced through the first reformed Legislative Council against government opposition. In almost all cases the government failed to implement the resolutions.[51] When the Nationalists introduced one resolution embodying their political

37

aspirations the government took a hands-off attitude, since it considered the matter "academic."[52]
The British policy for the development of self-rule
in Burma, which had been in advance of Burmese political opinion in 1917, failed to meet the aspirations of even the more moderate of the nationalist
intelligentsia in 1923 when it was finally implemented.

British policy was even further removed from
the demands of the extreme nationalists who reached
into the villages and raised a barrier of noncooperation against the government. The GCBA, and
particularly that bloc which followed U Ottama and
U Chit Hlaing, worked through the village wunthanu
athins. The economic disequilibrium following
World War I increased the economic difficulties
of the Burmese peasant. The ensuing agrarian discontent increased the proclivity of the villager
for political agitation, civil unrest, and illegal
actions.

The Crime Enquiry Committee of 1923 found that
the majority of robbers and dacoits (brigands) were
agricultural laborers and advanced the conclusion
that one of the major causes of crime was the
failure of wages to keep pace with rising living
costs.[53]   However, the ties of the cultivator to
the land were loosened by increases in tenancy,

38

agrarian debt, and land alienation. The influx of competitive Indian labor increased. The distraught Burmese peasant, beset by economic troubles, disturbed from his traditional mode of life, provoked by the absence or ineffectiveness of government attention to his welfare, and aroused by the *ponqyi* and the local *athin*, viewed the British administration as a major source of his troubles. The economic and social discontent of the Burmese peasant was exploited by the political opportunists among the nationalists. To the reformers these grievances suggested worthy objectives to be sought through legitimate political action.

Buddhism, as a major facet of the national identity of the Burmese, became intimately entwined with the popular concept of nationalism and was especially significant in bringing the villager into the nationalist movement. The agent for spreading the nationalist doctrine to the villages was the political *ponqyi*, who at once embodied the old respect for tradition and the new demand for self-determination.

The demands for prohibitions on the wearing of footwear in pagodas, for the removal of British military cantonments from the Shwe Dagon Pagoda area, and for the extension of the jurisdiction of the ecclesiastical head of the Burmese Buddhists were essentially religious issues that acquired nationalist overtones.[54] Agitation for home rule by U Ottama and other ponqyis were political demands, but the British administrators proceeded cautiously in such cases because government action against one ponqyi was regarded as an affront to the whole Buddhist religion.

The nationalist movement provided a means whereby the politically ambitious among the ponqyis might attempt to regain their political prestige. Their Buddhist monastic order, which had enjoyed an important position under the Burmese kings and had resisted the coming of British rule in 1852 and 1886, could exercise no direct influence on the British administration. The Buddhist order nominally became subject to the British courts, while the traditional ecclesiastical organs of monastic discipline fell away. The increasing political activities of some ponqyis were a pressing concern of the Burma government.[55]

Elements among the ponqyis organized the General Council of Sangha Sametgyis (coalition of ponqyi associations) in 1921 and "threw in its lot with the extremists and ere long (1925) dominated their activities."[56] Local branches of the General Council of Sangha Sametgyis were established, usually by the younger monks. The Sangha Sametgyis

40

were of great importance in the implementation of the boycott resolutions of the GCBA. In one case, ninety villagers met and resolved to have no religious association with a fellow villager because he had been "excommunicated" by the local ponqyi and his neighborhood Sangha.[57] The General Council of Sangha Sametgyis also participated in the boycott of the Prince of Wales.[58]

The ponqyi was the most important instrument by which the nationalist movement reached the villager and thereby gained wider support among the population. The HPG Party received the support of many of the ponqyis who exercised influence in the villages. These monks were instrumental in the development of the noncooperation movement among the local athins.[59] The villager was not only harangued by his ponqyi upon the vices of British rule, the dangers to Buddhism from foreign influences, and the resulting necessity for boycott, but were told that U Ottama had made an alliance with the King of France[60] and that America was ready with men and money to aid Burma to gain home rule.[61] More restrained appeals by other monks urged the people to cultivate national strength through wealth, knowledge, courage, and unity.[62]

The village wunthanu athins, active in the noncooperation movement of 1921-1922, developed

more aggressive inner societies called bu athins in
1923.[63] The purpose of these was to widen noncooperation with the government by such measures as the
refusal to pay taxes and the boycotting of elections. The athins attempted to supress the legal
sale and use of opium and intoxicating liquor and
to have the leased fisheries released from governmental control. Attempts were made to coerce non-
members to join the athins.[64]

The bu athins were declared illegal associations on August 2, 1923, and 303 athins of various
types had been declared unlawful by 1927 although
only 101 were still under the ban at that time.[65]
In Tharrawaddy District, where the movement was
strong, there were 730 members in 10 athins banned
in October, 1924.[66] The leaders or "managers"
were usually men of only local political importance.
A type of interlocking directorate probably existed
in some villages linking the athin and the Sangha
Sametgyis, since pongyis were listed among athin
leaders.[67]

Intimidation of officials and those who cooperated with the government continued, as did the
"shadow administrations" set up by some of the
athins. The old Burmese method of settling disputes
by mediation was revived and for a time at least
this practice was tolerated by the government,

42

whose court system was already overtaxed.[68]

Sibwaye athins (development associations) were
organized in Tharrawaddy District to intimidate the
Indian Chettyar moneylenders into reducing the debts
owed by the peasants. Those Chettyars who resisted
were boycotted, as were the villagers who refused
to join the sibwaye athin. The athins sometimes
used violence to enforce the boycotts.[69]

The thugyi had lost much of his effectiveness
as a result of the reorganization of the system of
rural government at the end of the nineteenth century. The activities of the athins further isolated
the headman from the community, since he could not
openly join an association opposing the government.
The thugyi's position became especially precarious
during the campaigns against the payment of taxes
beginning in 1924. When one zealous thugyi up-
braided some pongyis for attacking the government
in speeches, he was "excommunicated."[70] By undermining the authority of the thugyis, the nationalist
leaders disrupted the whole administrative system.
These minor officials, held responsible from above
and obstructed from below, suffered discomfort,
annoyance, social pressure, and physical violence
in attempting to discharge their functions.[71]
Often the thugyis went through the forms to satisfy
their superiors in the government while turning

43

their heads when the forms were ignored by the villagers. In an attempt to strengthen the waning authority of the _thuqyi_ and to eliminate the anti-government attitude of the _athins_, the Burma government sponsored official village associations in 1924, but these groups, set up to try petty cases and advise the _thuqyi_, failed to develop organic connections in the village communities.[72]

Violence in nationalist agitation took on a variety of forms. Crops were destroyed, cattle maimed, and assault, arson, and murder were committed. Certain of the _bu_ _athins_ were known as _luthat_, or murder associations. With the break-down of social controls and the increase of economic distress, it became increasingly difficult to dis-tinguish between the opportunistic criminal and the violent nationalist.[73] The problem of combating crime became more difficult when _athin_ members pledged not to give evidence to the police. How-ever, political agitation did not contribute to the increase in serious crime directly so much as it abetted crime by undermining the position of the _thuqyi_, bringing the government into con-tempt and creating "a general feeling of lawless-ness."[74]

The nonpayment of taxes was another method of obstructionism used by the nationalists that

44

persistently hampered the operation of the British administration in one of its most vulnerable areas-- revenues. The deliberate refusal to pay certain taxes, advocated by nationalist leaders, augmented the mounting revenue collection problems arising out of the ineffectiveness of village administration and out of the agrarian unrest. The Paungde Conference of the GCBA in May, 1924, called for the nonpayment of the capitation tax, a head levy imposed in Lower Burma. By June the thugyis in the rice-growing delta area were meeting resistance in collecting the capitation tax.[75] The nationalists of the HPG Party heralded the no-tax movement as a means for gaining home rule. The pongyis spread tales that the British would now be forced to leave Burma.[76] In October, 1924, Governor Sir Harcourt Butler made a tour of the disturbed area and concluded that the motive for the nonpayment of taxes was political and not economic.[77] The movement spread through five districts in Lower Burma, and, in several cases, the thugyi was murdered in the discharge of his duties as tax collector. In 1923-1924 coercive measures were required to collect Rs. 2,802,000 of taxes in arrears. By June, 1925, "the organized campaign of nonpayment of capitation tax (had) added seriously to the task of collection and rendered necessary coercive measures of all kinds on an unprecedented scale."[78] The Legislative Council was another arena in the nationalist campaign against the capitation tax and its counterpart in Upper Burma, the thathemada, or household tax. A committee investigated the operation of these two taxes in 1927 and recommended that they be abolished or, if that were not feasible, that the revenue be utilized for local purposes. The government did not implement the recommendations.[79] While the nonpayment campaign had receded by 1926, there was a recrudescence of the movement in 1927. The antitax program spread to Upper Burma where the thathemada levy was opposed. The government, armed with the experience gained in 1924, was able to put down the movement with greater efficiency. However, the capitation and thathemada taxes continued to be a source of discontent and an issue which the nationalists could exploit in their contest with the government. These antagonisms exacerbated relations between the government and the people of Burma and impeded the policy of developing self-rule.

CHAPTER 3

THE MOVEMENT FOR SEPARATION FROM INDIA
AND CONSTITUTIONAL REFORM

The leaders of the Burmese nationalist movement
differed as to the means and the timing of their
campaign for attaining self-rule. Should the
Burmese cripple British plans for gradual political
development by refusing to serve in the legislature
and local government bodies? Would it serve nationalist ends better to accept public office and
attempt to expand the role of Burmese in the government? Should Burma remain a part of India? Could
Burma achieve dominion status gradually or was
immediate home rule the only sure method of gaining
a government responsible to the people? Sincere
differences of opinion on such questions and the
personal ambitions of some nationalist leaders
impeded the consolidation of the nationalist
movement.

A further split in the GCBA over the issue of
the nonpayment of taxes was avoided only through
compromise at the Paungde Conference of May, 1924.
"Home rule" remained the goal of the GCBA, though
the unity of this body was now more in doubt. U

Ottama expressed the opinion of the more self-searching nationalists:

> We have not yet done sufficient work to inspire confidence in the people with our energy, our intelligence and our public spirit. We are groping in the dark and do not know what to do. Our organizations are idle and they have not yet begun to do constructive work.[1]

The All-Burma Union, an ephemeral political grouping, met at Mandalay in August, 1924, and attempted to prevent the splintering of the GCBA and to bring that group and the Nationalist Party together. The HPG Party convened a meeting in Mandalay at the same time to counter this attempt at compromise by the All-Burma Union. U Ottama, the spiritual leader of the HPG Party, headed a procession in Mandalay that clashed with the police, presumably over some confusion in routes. Several persons were killed. As a result eighteen nationalist leaders were arrested including Tun Aung Gyaw, one of the triumvirate of the HPG Party.[2] In October, U Ottama was again imprisoned for sedition, this time for a three-year term. Protest meetings, disorders, and a general unrest ensued.[3] The British policy of tutelage for self-rule was unacceptable to the more radical nationalists, while

48

repression of nationalist agitation by the government only bred further agitation. The Burma
government was continually faced with this dilemma
in dealing with the Burmese nationalists and in
carrying out its policy of gradual development of
self-rule.

The All-Burma Union was a last gesture at
nationalist unification before the 1925 Legislative
Council elections. The attempt by pongyis to control the HPG Party and prevent participation in the
election led to a breakup, and the pongyis formed
a separate GCBA under U Soe Thein. The Hlaing
group decided to form a Home Rule Party outside
their GCBA to campaign for seats in the Legislative
Council under the leadership of Tharrawaddy U Pu.
The strategy called for winning seats in the legislature and the "wrecking" the government from within. U Tok Kyi, who had been exposed to Indian
political influences, formed a Swaraj Party, so
that in the 1925 elections three nationalist
parties were in the field.

The Nationalist Party again won the largest
number of elected seats, but the bloc of minority
and special interest representatives, officials,
and conservative Burmese Council members banded
into the Independent and Golden Valley parties to
provide the government with a majority in the

49

Council. The Swaraj Party fell apart after a severe
defeat in the elections. With the dropping of the
boycott by elements of the GCBA and greater popular
interest, 16 percent of the voters participated in
the election.[4]

Obstructionism became more prominent in the
1925 Legislative Council. Several important
Nationalist Party members switched to the Independent Party, which supported the government, and
one member, Ba Yin, became Minister of Education.
The Home Member, U May Oung, formed the Independent
Party into what was in effect a ministerial party.
The Independent and Golden Valley parties plus the
official bloc assured the government's majority in
the Legislative Council. The nationalist opposition
consisted of the Swaraj, Home Rule, and Nationalist
parties which joined together to form the People's
Party in February, 1927. The more militant
attitude of the opposition was demonstrated by the
three walkouts staged in the Legislative Council.
When the government refused to abolish the post of
Development Commissioner in March, 1926, these
three parties left the chamber. Similar action
followed an alleged affront to U Ottama, and again
when a charge was leveled at the administration for
stiffling the opposition. Resolutions to increase
grants to the national schools, to appoint a Politi-

cal Prosecutions Standing Committee, to provide
for the election of thugyis, and to halt the
collection of the capitation and thathemada taxes
were defeated by the government supporters during
the second council. The growing nationalism of the
opposition was also indicated by the increase in
communal issues, especially with regard to the Indian minority.[5] The antagonisms between the nationalists and the government during the sessions of the
second Legislative Council impaired efforts to
broaden the legislative experience of the Burmese
in preparation for self-rule. However, the nationalists undoubtedly gained in political experience
and confidence from their confrontations with the
government in the Legislative Council.

In the rural areas the antitax campaign flared
up periodically to harass the administration. With
the renewal of the antitaxation program and the
resumption of activities by the newly freed U
Ottama in 1927, the government was faced with general unrest once again. "Strong measures" were taken
to check incipient disturbances in Tharrawaddy and
other districts. At the end of 1927, there was
"extreme tension" in four districts. Resistance
to the payment of the thathemada, or household tax,
grew in Upper Burma. An abortive uprising, led by
an obscure hermit, foreshadowed the rebellion of

51

1931-1932.[6]

The impending reexamination of the government
by the Indian Statutory (Simon) Commission produced
increased political activity, especially in the
organization of groups to champion the varying
nationalist points of view before the Parliamentary
investigators. Attempts to form a Unity League
based on a common program failed in 1928. The
question of separation from India now loomed larger
as India moved toward the goal of self-rule. For
many nationalists, Burma's position as a province
of an India that exercised effective self-government would be untenable. The fundamental distrust
of British policy led other nationalist groups to
combat separation because of the suspicion that
Burma, cut loose from the juggernaut of Indian
nationalism, would be denied political benefits
granted to India and turned into a crown colony.

The Burma for the Burmans League was formed
in July, 1928, to work for separation and dominion
status. Irked at the proposals of this new league
for the control of ponqyis, the politically active
monks formed a Hundred Committee to boycott the
Simon Commission, oppose separation, and gain
implicit obedience to the priests in all matters.
Another group, the Separation League, formed in
September, 1928, attempted to convene an All-

52

Parties Conference in December to consider a draft constitution but only those favoring separation took an active role.[7]

The third election to the reformed Legislative Council in 1928 saw the inevitable new political party. This group, the National Parliamentary Organization, after gaining five seats in the election, merged with the People's Party. The primary cleavage in the nationalist movement was between those who participated in the government and those who persisted in the boycott of the legislature. Those nationalists who entered the Legislative Council tended to stand together as in the case of the National Parliamentary Organization. The Independent Party won only twelve seats, a decline of eight, but still comprised the second largest bloc. The People's Party, successor to the Nationalist Party, again emerged with a plurality of elected seats. In all, the nationalist opposition won forty-five seats including those gained by the National Parliamentary Organization. However, a consolidation of the Independent Party votes with those of the official and nominated members denied the ministerial posts to the People's Party, which remained in opposition. The nationalist bloc did succeed in defeating Sir Oscar de Glanville, leader of the Independents, for the presidency of the

Legislative Council, electing U Pu by a margin of 44 to 41.[8] In essence, the Burmese nationalists in the Legislative Council had the opportunity to criticize the government without the sobering influence of sharing the responsibilities for government policy and administration.

In the rural areas unrest and crime persisted, especially in Tharrawaddy, where disturbances early in 1928 caused a reimposition of restrictions on village athins. Unknown to the Criminal Investigation Department of the Burma Police, the groundwork for the 1931-1932 rebellion was being laid in this district.

The religious aspect of the nationalist movement returned to plague the administration with the hunger strike of U Wizaya, a monk who was arrested for sedition in 1929. U Wizaya succumbed after a prolonged fast while in prison. The question of the treatment of imprisoned pongyis became the issue of the day. Although no incidents immediately followed U Wizaya's death, some five thousand persons participated in the cremation ceremony for this monk who was regarded as a martyr by his countrymen.[9]

As the time for the visit of the Simon Commission grew closer the unreconcilable nationalists unfurled the boycott banner again as they had in

54

1921 with the Whyte Committee. A Provincial Committee to consult with the Simon Commission was elected by the Burma Legislative Council but with progovernment forces in control of the legislature and nationalists refusing to participate, this committee included only "safe" Burmese and representatives of the minority groups. Those Burmese who favored separation saw Sir John Simon's group as a means to their end and cooperated in the inquiry. Those who opposed immediate separation from India organized a boycott of the commission. The Sangha Sametgyis GCBA was especially active in the boycott movement. Black banners enscribed "Simon Go Back" greeted the British parliamentarians upon their arrival and an All-Parties Simon Boycott Committee was formed. The Indian interests supported this attempt to forestall separation. Although the British investigators were cut off from official contact with the Burmese nationalists, many of their attitudes and ideas filtered through to the Simon Commission. Here again, full consideration of constitutional advance for Burma was hampered by the mutual suspicions of the administration and the more zealous nationalists.[10]

Nationalism expressed itself in hostility toward the Indian minority as well as toward the government. In May, 1930, serious Indo-Burmese

riots in Rangoon resulted in over a hundred
deaths.[11] Clearly unbridled nationalism in such a
destructive form would only complicate the task of
gradually shifting the responsibility of governing
Burma to the Burmese.

Soon after the Rangoon riots of 1930, a group
of ardent young nationalists formed the Dobama, or
"We Burmans" society, to intensify the nationalist
drive. Although it had only a limited following
at its inception, this group proved to be the source
of the nationalist leadership, which assumed control
in the final surge leading to Burma's independence.
The members of the Dobama society ironically took
the title of thakin, or "master" which had heretofore been a respectful term of address for
Europeans.[12]

Split over the issues of participation in the
government and separation from India, the various
nationalist parties, groups, blocs, and coteries in
the Burmese political arena maneuvered and shifted,
thrust and withdrew, seeking to gain political
leadership. Those policy makers and officials in
the British administration who strove to have the
Burmese share in their own government were harrassed
by the noncooperators, needled by those Burmese who
participated in political activities and impeded by
British officials and business interests who could

56

not or would not envisage responsible government.

While the Westernized Burmese leaders worked
for an increased role in the government in Rangoon,
a group of unknown men in the rural areas was shaping a plot to overthrow the British regime by force
of arms. Grievances stemming from the capitation
tax, agrarian indebtedness, and government orders
reserving timber areas and denying to the villagers
access to firewood were widespread in rural areas.
The U Soe Thein faction of the GCBA appointed a
committee under one Saya San, a former pongyi, to
investigate these problems. After this inquiry into
agrarian problems was completed, Saya San apparently
withdrew from the GCBA and in 1928 began to form
secret associations to resist forcibly the collection of the capitation tax. This effort broadened
into a movement for the overthrow of British power
in Burma. The center of the gathering storm was
in the upper delta district of Tharrawaddy, which
had been the center of resistance to taxation in
1927-1928. Saya San and his associates, appealing
to traditional Burmese political and religious beliefs, organized a rudimentary apparatus for rebellion in three of the delta districts. On October
28, 1930, Saya San was proclaimed king with the
title Thupannaka Galon Raja and established a
"court" in Tharrawaddy, all unknown to the govern-

ment.[13] Cadres for a rebel army with uniforms but few arms were formed into regiments, drilled, and indoctrinated for the coming struggle.[14] The Westernized Burmese leaders were not involved in this affair although undoubtedly some GCBA leaders were cognizant of developments in the villages. The British Governor, Sir Charles Innes, was in Great Britain, and Sir Joseph Maung Gyi was acting as the head of the government, the first Burmese to hold the office. While on tour through Tharrawaddy on December 21, Sir Joseph refused to grant a petition for reduced taxation which was presented to him by the local peasants.

The Saya San forces launched their rebellion the next day, December 22. The initial effort by the rebels was to gain arms. Villages were attacked and the headmen's guns and other weapons were seized.[15] The Rangoon government failed to appreciate the potential strength of this movement and matters soon were out of control. Troops were deployed, yet the rebellion spread. By January the rebel organization had launched campaigns in other districts, some of which were quickly smashed. With the deployment of British troops in the field, the rebels abandoned open confrontation for guerrilla tactics. The _pongyis_ were instrumental in the spread of the rebellion through much of Lower Burma

58

and the Shan States. Numerous village _athins_ as
well as the U Soe Thein GCBA were outlawed. Although in mid-February, 1931, the rebellion was
officially declared to be a problem which the police
could now handle, troops continued to be employed.
The peak of the outbreak was reached by May and
June, 1931, but order was restored only gradually.
Dacoity and rebellion often became indistinguishable
as criminals took advantage of the breakdown of law
and order to terrorize the villages.

The Secretary of State for India announced
that the government's policy was "to endow the local
Governor with whatever power and force he considers
necessary but at the same time to pursue diligently
the treatment both of economic and political forces
which appear to be at the root of the trouble."[16]
A special commissioner was appointed to coordinate
the civil and military efforts in the five districts
where the rebellion centered. A bill to constitute
special tribunals to handle the trials of the rebels
was defeated by the legislature in Rangoon. The
Governor, Sir Charles Innes, who had hurried back
from Britain when the proportions of the uprising
became known, used his special powers to certify
the bill as law. These special tribunals provided
summary trials without jury but with the right of
appeal to a higher court.

In August, 1931, the government offered amnesty to all rebels except the leaders and those who actively participated in major incidents. Amnesty was granted to those who pledged to return to their home villages and to give information on other rebels.[17] "Peace missions" were formed by certain pongyis who visited the villages attempting to calm the upheaval. The number who accepted the government's offer of amnesty grew in the final months of 1931. In November the instigator of the rebellion, Saya San, was executed. One important gang evaded the government until April, 1932. By June, 1932, Burma had returned to a state of relative order after eighteen months of revolt and chaos.

The rebellion had little or no immediate effect on the development of new political institutions and arrangements for Burma. It did, however, reveal something of the depth of Burmese national feeling rooted in traditional institutions and folkways. The actions of the rebels, poorly armed but often courageous, generated a surge of national pride among many Burmese.[18] The rebellion also forcefully focussed attention on the shocking conditions of tenancy, indebtedness, and economic depression in rural areas.

The rebellion also had its impact on the Westernized political leadership. Burmese in the

Legislative Council and the London Round Table Conference, reflecting popular sympathy for the rebels,
attempted to gain more lenient treatment for them.
Two lawyers, Dr. Ba Maw and U Saw, volunteered to
defend Saya San, and the case provided a spring-
board to political prominence for both men.

The Simon Commission's recommendation that
Burma be separated from India was subject to still
greater suspicion among the nationalists when no
antiseparationists were selected to serve on the
Burma delegation to the Indian Round Table Conference (1930) on constitutional reform. When a resolution calling for the termination of Burma's ties
with India was slipped through the Indian Round
Table Conference, these doubts of the nationalists
mounted. The participation of the antiseparationists in the Burma Round Table Conference gave full
voice to the demands of the Burmese nationalists
and brought out the "popular lack of confidence"
in the British regime in Burma.[19] The Burmese
delegates, though diverging in their proposals
for instruments of government, were agreed that
dominion status was needed to assure responsible
government in Burma.[20]

Another attempt was made to consolidate the
three GCBA groups. A joint conference was held at
Mandalay in October-November, 1930, and although

a resolution was signed announcing unification, there remained the old division on the issue of participating in the government or maintaining the boycott. Three of the GCBA factions at the Mandalay meeting, however, agreed strongly on opposing separation from India, insisting that Burma be offered full dominion status first. Subsequently, the Indian National Congress at its Karachi meeting (March-April, 1931) and the India Legislative Council (March, 1932) supported the position that Burma was entitled to remain part of India with the right of withdrawal, thus directly challenging British policy. Opposition to separation from India finally provided common ground for briefly uniting major dissident elements in the GCBA into the Anti-Separationist League in July, 1932, apparently with the backing and encouragement of influential Indians. These elements of the GCBA abandoned their policy of refusing participation in the dyarchy government of Burma and launched a vigorous election campaign in 1932, by cooperating in the Anti-Separationist League.[21]

The impending election of 1932 was viewed by the London government as a popular referendum on the separation issue. Observers of Burmese opinion felt reasonably certain that the proseparation candidates would be returned. However, the anti-

62

separationists, who had usually boycotted previous
elections, now organized in the Anti-Separationist
League and entered the contest for the Legislative
Council. U Ba Pe's People's Party and the Independent Party of Joseph Maung Gyi, both advocating
separation, were favored to win. However, the Anti-
Separationist League captured forty-two seats while
the separationists won only twenty-nine, nine going
to neutrals.[22] The proseparation forces accused
the victors of deceiving the electorate with lurid
previews of alleged intolerable conditions in a
separated Burma and of utilizing Indian funds to
manipulate the elections.

Both the British policy makers and Burmese
separationists refused to accept the ostensible
mandate given at the polls for federation with
India, and consideration of Burma's future status
was shifted to the newly elected Legislative
Council. Dr. Ba Maw, a rising nationalist leader,
U Chit Hlaing and their respective factions in the
Anti-Separationist League persisted in their some-
what different demands for federation with India
with the option of withdrawal. This course of
action was clearly precluded in the policy statement by the Prime Minister at the conclusion of
the Burma Round Table Conference. A ministerial
interregnum ensued for a short period when the

leaders of the major parties in the Legislative Council refused to accept either of the two ministerial positions in charge of transferred subjects. After a brief controversy ridden ministry that included the Independent Joseph Maung Gyi and Kyaw Din, a lieutenant of Ba Maw, both Ba Pe and Ba Maw relented and assumed the offices they maintained until 1936, though they disagreed on the separation issue.[23] The Legislative Council was deeply enmeshed in the separation controversy. During the parliamentary maneuverings on a resolution for conditional federation the President of the Council, U Chit Hlaing, was removed from his position, following a bitter controversy over a ruling he had made. His successor, Sir Oscar de Glanville, who was a European of the Independent Party, experienced increasing difficulty with the nationalist members of the Legislative Council and, after a prolonged struggle, was removed from office by the Governor in 1935 at the insistence of the majority of the Council members.[24] U Chit Hlaing was then returned to the presidency of the Legislative Council.

The focus of nationalist attention again shifted to London where Parliament's Joint Committee on Indian Constitutional Reform was in session. After discussions with the leading Burmese nationalists the committee inferred, in effect, that the

64

antiseparationists were motivated by suspicion of British intent and that they ultimately desired separation under their own terms. On this basis, the committee recommended that if separation was to be carried out, it should not be postponed.[25]

The Burmese nationalists during the early part of this period prior to World War II were primarily concerned with a political issue--gaining as great a degree of self-government as possible. Economic grievances were used to weight the arguments for political self-determination since the latter would presumably offer the means for redressing these grievances. In the 1930s, however, Marxist ideology became more prevalent among the new leaders who were emerging. At the Burma Round Table Conference the attack on imperialism by two Burmese national-ists carried Marxist overtones. The police adminis-tration expressed concern about the hold of communism on the minds of Burma's youth. Though Marxism was still confined to propaganda, the apprehensive Inspector-General of Police considered communism a "real danger to the government."[26] The thakins of the Dobama society were the principal political group conversant with Marxist dogma. In 1935 the Dobama absorbed the embryonic All-Burma Youth League to form the Dobama Asi Ayon (We Burmans Association). This organization in turn

formed a political party, the Komin Kochin (One's
Own King, One's Own Kind), in 1936 to contest the
first election after the passage of the Government
of Burma Act, 1935. The Dobama Asi Ayon drew many
of its leaders from the student movement. Aung
San was President of the All-Burma Party in 1939.[27]

The student movement became intensely nationalistic and in 1936, the thakins won control of the
Executive Council of the Rangoon University Student
Union. Budding nationalist leaders at Rangoon University such as Thakin Aung San and Thakin Nu worked
to make the students aware of agrarian problems as
well as political issues. Six hundred students
staged a strike in February, 1936, and left Rangoon
University just before the examination period. The
strike, sparked by orders expelling Thakin Nu from
the university and disciplining Thakin Aung San for
criticisms of the university system, broadened into
a general attack on the University Act of 1920.
Agitation for amendments to the act to make the
university administration more responsive to public
opinion dragged on until 1939 when changes, which
met most of the demands of the students and Burmese
political leaders, were made.[28] The Rangoon University strike of 1936 proved to be the initial
major political action undertaken by young leaders
who would bring independence to Burma.

66

The elections of November, 1936, were held to
determine the membership of the new legislature under the Government of Burma Act which was to come
into force the next year. These groups, which had
opposed separation so stubbornly, quickly accepted
the new status of Burma after 1935 and accommodated
their policies to the new situation. As yet there
was little real attention to party platforms and
candidates usually stood as members of coteries
grouped about a well-known leader or as a representative of minority interests. Ba Maw's Sinyetha
(Proletarian's) Party had the most elaborate program, calling for a five-year plan for village
reconstruction and agrarian reform.[29] The more
nationalistic Thakin or Komin Kochin Party sounded
the familiar call for self-rule while demanding a
greater role for the Burmese in the economic life
of the country. U Ba Pe and his People's Party
formed a coalition with four other political factions, the Ngabwinsaing, or Five Groups Alliance
Party. The progovernment Independent Party and
the Chit Hlaing group also nominated candidates.
The Ngabwinsaing Party won 46 of the 132 seats in
the new House of Representatives. The Sinyetha
group captured sixteen seats, the Independents
seventeen, and the Chit Hlaing coterie twelve.
The new thakin group seated only three of its

67

candidates.[30]   Ba Pe was unable to form a ministry
and relinquished the country's leadership to Ba Maw
who formed a precarious coalition which depended
on the support of the Europeans and other minority
representatives.

CHAPTER 4

THE DEVELOPMENT OF POLITICAL INSTITUTIONS

British policy makers and the Western-educated Burmese nationalists emphasized the institutional aspects of the political development of Burma. Separation from India, the transfer of power to responsible ministers, and the representation of minorities
were among the many problems of this type which persisted throughout this period of political development.

The British officials who helped to shape the
political evolution of Burma sought to devise a
legislature and an executive that could invest Burma with the forms of responsible government while
preserving what they considered to be adequate safeguards to ensure the unimpaired economic development of the country. The fundamental dilemma in the
development of political institutions for Burma
remained unsolved. How could sufficient authority
to permit effective action and to instill political
responsibility be delegated to the Burmese while
the ultimate power of decision making was retained
in the hands of the experienced British administrator?

In 1917 Burma was a province of India under
the rule of the Governor-General in New Delhi, who
was in turn responsible to the Secretary of State
for India in London. The provincial government was
administered by the Lieutenant-Governor of Burma
assisted by a small Legislative Council. This body,
formed in 1897, though not so devised, was the
prototype for the representative legislature that
evolved in Burma.[1] From an original membership of
five European officials, two nonofficial Europeans,
one nonofficial Burmese, and one Shan chief nominated by the Governor, the Legislative Council had
grown to fifteen (1909) and then to seventeen
(1915)--two members of whom were elected, one by
the Burma (British) Chamber of Commerce and one
by the Rangoon Trades Association.

The 1897 Legislative Council had limited
powers to pass local laws subject to tight restrictions. Power to discuss the province's annual
financial statement and other matters of public
interest and to interrogate officials was gained
in 1909. The legislature did not vote the budget,
however. In 1920 the membership was increased to
thirty, including the two elected representatives
of the British commercial interests. The non-
officials who were usually of the propertied class
included ten natives of Burma, two Indians, and a

Chinese. The reforms of the Legislative Council prior to 1923 were based on the necessities of administrative decentralization. The direct participation of the business community in the governing process was one significant outcome of these reforms.[2]

The policy statement by the Secretary of State for India, Sir Edwin Montagu, on August 20, 1917, pledging the British government to "the gradual developing of self-governing institutions with a view to the progressive realization of responsible government in India as an integral part of the British Empire" provided the general criteria for the reform of the political machinery in Burma.[3]

Even in the initial stages of the investigation of political reform for India made by the Secretary of State, Sir Edwin Montagu, and the Viceroy, Lord Chelmsford, Burma's peculiar problems were recognized. The members of the Burma deputation, which presented their demands to Montagu and Chelmsford in Calcutta, December, 1917, impressed the Secretary of State with their "complete loyalty," freedom from political unrest, and desire for separation from India. Montagu's initial proposal called for a separate Burma under the Viceroy as Governor of India and Burma with financial autonomy except for imperial defense contributions. Although the Home

Member of the Indian government "liked" Montagu's
Burma proposals, they were apparently dropped and
not included in the final report.[4] The recommendations by Montagu and Chelmsford proceeded on the
premise that the earlier steps to be taken in the
progressive realization of responsible government
should be on the provincial level, where as complete responsibility "as conditions permit" should
be given. However, Burma was excluded from the
general proposals for the Indian provinces, and
the question of its political future was set aside
for "separate and future consideration." The
report argued that "Burma is not India," yet for
military reasons it must remain a part of India.
The stage of Burma's political development differing from India's, the report concluded that "the
way is open for a different line of development."[5]

Since the recommendations of the Viceroy and
Secretary of State excluded Burma from the general
reforms for India, Burma's Governor, Sir Reginald
Craddock, was empowered to develop separate proposals for Burma. He submitted these to the government of India in June, 1919, after informal discussions with a limited number of interested parties in
Burma. The heart of this plan, known as the "Craddock Scheme," was a system of four boards, three
of which, dealing with home affairs, revenue and

finance, and local self-government, could be headed by Burmese who, in effect, would have limited authority but would be trained as ministers. These boards and the Governor would form the executive side of the provincial government. In this "scheme of training" the extension of powers and responsibilities to the Burmese was to be "a matter of slow development."[6] The Craddock proposals called for a wide measure of local self-government and a Legislative Assembly with a "substantial majority" of elected members. Elections to the Legislative Assembly were to be direct, except for rural representatives who were to be elected by local government bodies. Separation from India was to be the ultimate goal of the reforms.[7]

Protracted consultations between Rangoon, New Delhi, and London about the structure of the reformed government and the degree to which Burmese should participate in the administration ensued for three years. The Indian government criticized Craddock's system of boards as unmanagable and inadequate. Nevertheless the boards were retained in a modified form in the revised proposal by the Burma government in January, 1920. Craddock was called to New Delhi to iron out differences in opinion on reform. A "joint" scheme was consequently forwarded to London in March, 1920, which

was in essence the Indian government's plan. [Citing
the political inexperience of the Burmese, the proposals advocated some control of the administration
by Burmese officials but no immediate ministerial
responsibility.] The boards were rejected and an
Executive Council of six with departmental committees was to be established to train Burmese, since
none were deemed capable of serving as executive
councilors. Wide extension of local self-government and an increase in the number of directly
elected members of the Legislative Council were
other features of this joint proposal by the
governments of India and Burma.[8]

Meanwhile in Great Britain the Parliamentary
Joint Select Committee on the Government of India
Bill heard U Pu, a representative of the Burma Reform League, condemn the Craddock Scheme and press
for the inclusion of Burma in the Government of
India Act.[9] The committee showed little interest
in this testimony and recommended the exclusion of
Burma from the reforms without clearly setting forth
their reasons. However, this parliamentary body
felt that Burma deserved and "should receive a constitution analogous to that provided in this /Gov-
ernment of India7 Bill. . . ."[10] When the Government of India Bill was considered in Commons in
December, 1919, a motion to include Burma was deba-

74

ted and withdrawn after assurances were given that Burma would receive "a real advance toward responsible government," although Montagu was unable to give a definite promise as to when a bill on Burma would be introduced.[11]

The government of India's plan for Burma, which had been worked out with Governor Craddock, was presented to Montagu in March, 1920. Various Burmese groups flooded Montagu with telegrams protesting that the New Delhi plan for Burma failed to meet the conditions of the Montagu Declaration of 1917 and the requirements for an "analogous" constitution set up by the Joint Select Committee.[12]

The Burmese nationalists despatched a second deputation to London in May, 1920, consisting of U Pu, U Ba Pe, and U Thein Maung. This group was assisted by a former member of the Indian Civil Service, Bernard Houghton, and an Indian, P. J. Mehta. The deputation realized that a demand for separation would delay the reforms and therefore asked that the Secretary of State utilize a special power contained in the Government of India Act (1919) to declare Burma a "Governor's province" by "notification" or executive order. By this process Burma would gain the constitutional advances granted to the other Indian provinces.[13] The Burma deputation placed its case before the special committee of Parliament considering Indian problems. Montagu himself objected to the government of India plan of March, since it made no provision for ministerial responsibility to the legislature. Montagu publicly admitted that there were differences between the India Office and the government of India as to the status of Burma.[14]

A committee of the Indian government investigated the financial relations between India and Burma. This was a sensitive matter and the subject of numerous differences between the central and provincial administrations. The investigating group, known as the Meston Committee, was particularly concerned about the financial status of Burma, since future revenue increases were largely discounted by heavy commitments needed to give the province the administrative facilities it lacked.[15] For these reasons Burma was to carry only 6-1/2 percent of the Indian debt. Nevertheless about 50 percent of the provincial revenues were surrendered to the central government.[16]

The political aspirations of the Young Burmans were reflected in a resolution adopted by the Burma Legislative Council on February 21, 1921. Introduced by Maung Chit Pe of the Young Burman group, the resolution demanded reforms at least equal to those granted to the major Indian provinces. The

76

debate in the council pointed up the growing impatience with the numerous delays in implementing the Montagu Declaration of 1917.[17]

The Parliamentary Standing Joint Committee on Indian Affairs accepted with some misgivings Montagu's proposal that the India Act (1919) be applied to Burma, feeling that prompt action was necessary. A committee to enquire into the special problems of the franchise, electorates, and the subjects to be transferred from the Governor to ministers was suggested.[18]

In November, 1921, a committee of the Indian government assembled in Rangoon with Frederick Whyte, an experienced member of the Indian Civil Service, as chairman, to "advise as to the rules which should now be made in order to apply the provisions of the Government of India Act relating to Governor's provinces, as modified by the notification, to Burma."[19] Although boycotted by the nationalists, this committee examined 101 witnesses, one-third of whom were officials. The primary concerns of the committee were the franchise, communal electorates, and the division of administrative subjects first between the central government and the province and secondly between the Governor of Burma and the ministers.

The Rangoon government had by this time aban-

doned the limited Craddock reforms and proposed a
wide electorate based on the payment of the capitation or the thathemada (household) taxes, which
would make about one of every six persons a voter.
The government was willing to eliminate communal
seats in the Legislative Council for Indians,
Chinese, and Karens as proposed by Craddock, leaving
only Europeans and Anglo-Indians in this special
category. [Though considering separation from India
inevitable, the Burma government was unwilling to
see the process evolve by gradually shifting
functions of the central government to the provincial level.] In transferring subjects from the
Governor to the ministers, the Burma government was
willing to go as far as the other major provinces,
but no farther.[20]

Since the more vigorous nationalists had boycotted the Whyte Committee, there was little nationalist sentiment displayed at the hearings.
Much time was given to pleading special interests
while the Burmese officials offered only minor
amendments to the government's proposals. The Burma (European) Chamber of Commerce endorsed the wide
electorate proposed by the government as did the
majority of British officials.

Faced with a general unanimity among the witnesses and in the evidence presented, the Whyte
78

Committee accepted in essence the proposals of the Burma government. A franchise for persons over eighteen years of age who paid either the capitation or _thathemada_ tax was endorsed by the committee. Though recognizing that communal electorates were theoretically undesirable, the committee proposed communal representation for Europeans and Anglo-Indians and the reservation of special seats in certain plural member constituencies for Indians and Karens. Elected members in the Legislative Council proposed by the Whyte Committee would total 78 as compared with the 66 proposed by the government, while the 23 nominated members would be 4 less than the total recommended by the government.

The committee was reluctant to propose changes in the division of administrative matters between India and Burma, since the process might cause further delay in the reforms. Contrary to the recommendations of the government, the committee was of the opinion that forestry, a key industry in Burma, should be transferred to a minister for administration, as should education.

The recommendations of the committee, presented in 1922, were accepted "to a great extent" by the government of India. New Delhi now moved to hold elections in Burma in November, 1922, so that the reforms might be implemented by the beginning of 1923 with the seating of a new Legislative Council.

Because of the disagreement which had marked the discussion of reforms for Burma, the rules regarding the franchise, constituencies, and the legislature, were submitted to Parliament in London, where they were debated at length. [Conservative members opposed the transfer of forests and the limited size of the constituency granted to Europeans and challenged the whole concept of constitutional advance for Burma.] A concerted effort was made by a Labor member, Colonel Wedgewood, to liberalize the rules relating to communal voting. As adopted by Parliament the rules granted to Burma greater constitutional gains than the other major Indian provinces in providing for the administration of forests and education by ministers and a broad suffrage.[21] The new constitutional machinery was activated on January 2, 1923, when Burma became a full-fledged governor's province under the so-called dyarchy system.[22] The reforms now faced the conclusive test of providing a viable system of government while promoting greater participation of the Burmese in the politics of their country.

The political powers in India were divided between the central and the provincial governments. Defense and foreign relations were functions of the

80

central administration, and, consequently, Burmese participating in the provincial government received no experience in administering these important matters. The provincial government in Burma under the 1923 reforms was characterized by a system of divided executive functions known as dyarchy, which had been devised for the other provinces of India under the Act of 1919. The two nominated members of the Governor's Executive Council administered "reserved" subjects; law and order, land revenue, finance, and labor being the most important. "Transferred" subjects, agriculture, excise, health, public works (except irrigation), and other "nation-building" functions were administered by two ministers selected by the Governor from among the members of the Legislative Council. In addition forests and education were transferred, which placed Burma in advance of other Indian provinces in this respect. The rationale of dyarchy was based on its flexibility, which theoretically would permit the gradual transfer of executive responsibility to the Burmese without prejudicing internal stability.[23]

The Legislative Council was expanded to include 103 members distributed as follows: of those nominated, 2 were serving ex officio (members of the Executive Council); 13 were officials; and 8 were nonofficials.

	Total
Elected	80
Nominated	23

The nominated nonofficials represented certain minorities and special economic interests. Elective constituencies were either general or assigned to minorities or special interests.

The Legislative Council could not make laws for the "backward tracts" generally inhabited by non-Burmese peoples, which were ruled directly by the Governor. This body was further prohibited from enacting legislation that would affect the distribution of powers within the existing framework of government. The Governor of Burma, the Governor-General of India, and the British cabinet all held veto powers. The Governor had the power to suspend consideration of a bill or to certify the passage of a bill relating to reserved subjects. The Legislative Council had limited budgetary powers. The Governor had sole power to propose expenditures and could override rejection or reduction of even that portion of the budget subject to Legislative Council approval by certifying that the expenditure was essential to the discharge of his responsibilities.[24] Questions, resolutions, and motions for adjournment were the means of inquiry and expression open to the Legislative Council.

The Instrument of Instruction issued to the
Governor on assuming his duties was another feature
designed to introduce flexibility into the government. These instructions set forth the policy
which the Governor should pursue during his term
of office. By adjusting the directions given to
successive Governors, an increasing role in the
government could be assigned to the Burmese as and
when the British policy makers saw fit.

Dyarchy, opposed in theory, now in practice became the target of increased nationalist criticism.
Proposals for further constitutional reform appeared
with increasing frequency. Typical of these programs was that put forward by the Home Rule Sub-
Committee of the All-Burma Union. The draft constitution called for dominion status, ministerial responsibility, and a noncommunal parliament.[25] The
Nationalist Party, led by U Pu, pushed a resolution
through the Legislative Council in 1924 recommending
sweeping changes in the distribution of governmental
powers. Carried by a vote of 41 to 23, the resolution envisaged the delegation of all the functions
of government to the provinces, except defense and
foreign relations. In turn all powers on the provincial level would be transferred to ministers
selected from the Legislative Council. The govern-

ment abstained from the discussions of these proposals, though the Burmese ministers joined their countrymen in supporting the resolution.[26]

The Government of India Act, 1919, provided for the appointment of a commission after ten years to enquire into the operation of the act and to make recommendations for constitutional reforms. Strong protests followed the decision in 1927 to restrict the personnel of the Indian Statutory Commission to members of Parliament. In an attempt to offset this criticism and to provide a group of Indians with whom the British commissioners could collaborate, an Indian Central Committee was selected from the Indian legislature in New Delhi. The committee, which visited Burma with the Indian Statutory Commission, had no members from Burma.

The committee hedged on the basic question of the separation of Burma from India. While recognizing the existence of a strong sentiment for separation in Burma, the committee did not feel able to recommend such a move until the financial and military relations with India were settled. The committee wished to shift the source of governmental powers to the provinces by making all subjects provincial except those specifically classified as central. Dyarchy would be abolished by ending the distinction between reserved and trans-

84

ferred subjects. Joint ministerial responsibility
vested in a cabinet of five, and the continuance of
communal representation were supported by the committee.[27] These advisory recommendations were only
designed to assist the parliamentary commission
reach its decision and were not incorporated in the
commission's report.

The Burma Provincial Committee was elected by
the Legislative Council to further assist the Indian
Statutory Commission with "the purpose of determining
the immediate steps necessary for the attainment of
full responsible government." Of the opinion that
"Burma's political subservience to India has seriously jeopardized her financial and economic interests and even threatens to denaturalize her," the
committee recommended separation.[28] Responsible
government would be promoted by establishing direct
relations with the government in Great Britain.
The proposals for legislative reform were moderate.
Communal electorates would be maintained, though
the majority of the committee favored a unicameral
legislature. The official bloc and nominated members would be eliminated only after a five-year period. The Governor under the scheme proposed by the
Burma Provincial Committee would act on the advice
of ministers but would retain emergency powers.
The six ministers would be jointly responsible to

the legislature. The most significant innovation proposed was the vesting of the power of constitutional amendment in the legislature subject to the approval of the Secretary of State for India and Burma. Since separation, on which the proposed reforms depended, was by no means a certainty, the committee recommended that should Burma remain a part of India, it should receive the same advances as granted to the major Indian provinces.[29]

The prevailing idea among officials and other British residents in Burma regarding separation was that the closer India approached responsible government, the more necessary it was to break Burma's connection with India, and avoid the possibility of Indians in New Delhi governing Burma. The government of Burma placed the case for separation before the Indian Statutory Commission, but averred that the decision to carry out the measure should be based on the desires of the people of Burma. Cognizant of the attitude of the Burmese nationalists, the government memorandum to the commission assumed that Burma would have a constitution that would "resemble in material particulars" that evolved for the central government in India.[30] On this basis, the government did not spell out recommendations for a constitutional system to the commission, waiting to see what reforms were proposed for India.

86

The outline of government proposed to the commission
by the Burma administration, if separation were not
recommended, emphasized the necessity for checks
and safeguards.[31]

The Indian Statutory Commission was exposed to
pleas and proposals from a wide range of opinion
in Burma. The British commercial groups were reluctant to see Burma fall behind the other Indian
provinces in reforms. The Burma Chamber of Commerce, while backing separation, was preoccupied
with establishing checks on any reformed government.
The retention of the official bloc in the Legislative Council, of British personnel in important
positions in the civil service, and the reservation
of seats for minorities and special interests in
the Legislative Council would give the security
the British interests required, the chamber of
commerce stated.

The numerous minority groups which presented
evidence to the commission were primarily concerned
with preserving and enlarging the number of communal
seats that they held in the Legislative Council.
Generally the Indian minority argued the antiseparationist case, while the Karens and Anglo-Indian
groups took the opposite side in this basic issue.
In terms of constitutional reform the minority demands ranged from dominion home rule, advocated by

87

the Karen National League, to a more cautious plea
for gradual development of self-governing institutions.[32]

The Burma for the Burmans League and the Separation League both submitted draft constitutions for
a Burma "Free State" as a self-governing dominion.
Reflecting Western institutional influences, the
proposed constitutions were characterized by minis-
tries responsible to popularly elected legislatures.
While granting the British governor the power to
withhold approval of a bill passed by the legislature, the draft constitutions proposed that this
body should have the power to initiate constitutional amendments. The separationists were the more
moderate of the nationalists, and their draft constitutions did not envisage sweeping changes but
rather a consolidation of Burma's political advances to that time under a unitary, responsible
government.[33]

The Statutory Commission adopted in large
measure the proposals of the government of Burma in
making its recommendations. While agreeing that
separation should take place "forthwith," the commission did not follow the Burma government in
assuming that the new constitution for Burma would
"resemble in material particulars" the pattern
adopted for India. Rather they distinguished Bur-

ma's problem as a special case to be decided on its own merits. Backward tracts and other special subjects must be withheld from popular control for, "The ultimate advancement of Burma will depend more than anything on the efficiency of a suitable administration during the years now coming, and premature efforts to dispense with help from Britain would only lead to disaster."[34]

The suspicions of the antiseparationist Burmese nationalists were strengthened by the position taken by the Statutory Commission emphasizing the limitations that should be placed on the grant of political powers made to a separated Burma. The appointment of only proseparationist delegates to represent Burma at the Indian Round Table Conference seemed to be part of a conspiracy to separate Burma from India and then deny any significant reforms. The Burma Sub-Committee of the Indian Round Table Conference, 1930-1931, was instructed "to consider the nature of the conditions which would enable Burma to be separated from India on equitable terms and to recommend the best way for securing this end."[35] The British chairman therefore would not permit general discussion on the merits of separation per se nor of the type of the constitution Burma should be given, though Indian members argued that it was not possible to discuss procedures for separation without delving into substantive matters. Lord Russell, chairman of the Burma Sub-Committee, assured the members that the prospects for Burma's constitutional advance would not be prejudiced by separation. The Burma Sub-Committee report called upon the British government to issue a statement accepting separation in principle without prejudice to Burma's prospects for gaining reforms. Again emphasis was placed on safeguarding minority rights. Other separation questions such as defense, financial settlements, and commerce should be farmed out to experts and agreed upon by India and Burma. The report was contested in the Committee of the Whole so that the report on Burma was merely "noted." In the final plenary session the Prime Minister stated that "the Government will pursue the decisions of that (Burma) sub-committee; separating Burma and making the necessary enquiries as to the conditions upon which the separation is to take place."[37]

The Burma Round Table Conference, which included antiseparationist delegates, convened in November, 1931, to discuss the lines of a constitution for a separated Burma. Tharrawaddy U Pu soon made it clear that the opponents of separation would leave the conference it if seemed likely that an unacceptable constitution would be forced on

90

Burma. The aspirations of the Burmese nationalists were symbolized by "Dominion Status" and "Home Rule" to be carried out in a constitution modeled on that of the Irish Free State. [The British delegates from Burma to the conference emphasized the necessity of gradualism and safeguards.]

A basic disagreement as to the conference procedures quickly arose and persisted throughout the discussions. The Burmese nationalists led by U Ba Pe and Tharrawaddy U Pu insisted that the British government make a policy statement setting out the degree of responsibility which the reformed Burma government was to exercise before any discussion of details was undertaken. Lord Peel, the chairman, attempted to avoid general discussions, emphasizing specific constitutional problems. He reasoned that the conference was called to help shape British policy for Burma and it would defeat the purpose of the Round Table Conference if the British placed a predetermined policy before the group.[38] Lord Peel did make a statement setting forth his impression of the general outline of Burma's future constitution. The conference should attempt, he stated, "to devise a constitution which will have in it the means of growth toward the declared goal of complete responsible government, but will contain provisions necessary to safeguard certain obligations and

interests."[39]   The antiseparationist Burmese headed
by U Chit Hlaing and Tharrawaddy U Pu, felt this
statement did not meet Burma's aspirations for
immediate and full responsible government with
dominion status and therefore refused to participate
further in the conference.[40]

The report which emerged from the turbulent
sessions of the Round Table Conference was in essence
a record of the opinions and the limited areas of
agreement of the various divergent interests present. Except for the more adamant advocates of full
responsible government, the delegates agreed
generally on the framework of a constitution that
would place upon a legislature of the peoples of
Burma the responsibility for the government of the
colony. The Governor would be vested with all the
necessary powers to discharge his regular duties as
well as to administer certain reserved subjects.
Yet attempts to specify which powers were "necessary"
for the Governor and which subjects should be reserved indicated the divergences between the British
power holders and the Burmese power seekers. Some
consensus was obtained on the projected Parliament
of Burma and it was generally agreed that ministerial
responsibility should obtain in the new government.

The difficulties to agreement presented by
differences in the basic premises of the British

92

policy makers and the Burmese nationalists were manifest throughout the discussions. The British saw the reforms in Burma as a gradual process of constitutional advance carefully hedged by safe-guards which would insure the best interests of all concerned. For their part the nationalists en-visaged the wholesale turnover of political power by the British, subject to unavoidable en-cumberances which would be shed as rapidly as possible.

The most significant result, which proceeded immediately from the round-table discussions, was a detailed policy statement by the Prime Minister made at the final session of the conference on January 12, 1932. The Prime Minister averred that the British government was ready, when satisfied that the people of Burma desired separation, to take steps to entrust the responsibility for the government of Burma to a representative legislature and responsible ministry subject, of course, to certain qualifications and conditions. This policy statement was in general accord with the concepts set forward by the Indian Statutory Com-mission. The first step would be to determine the Burmese attitude on separation now that the general nature of the proposed constitution had been set forth.

The British Parliament now undertook the long process of sifting the recommendations of the Simon Commission, the Round Table Conferences, and the India Office and evolving a constitutional statute for Burma. The Parliamentary Joint Committee on Indian Constitutional Reform accepted the white paper submitted by the Secretary of State for India as a basis for discussion. This document was in line with the proposals put forward by the Simon Commission. Burma would have a separate, unitary government consisting of a bicameral legislature and a governor assisted by ministers with limited powers. Despite the antiseparationist victory in the 1932 election, the committee felt that separation was justified in the light of the presumed objectives of Burmese nationalists as well as for practical administrative reasons. The Governor would serve as the instrument for exercising the "safeguards" and gradually expanding the responsibilities of Burma's legislators and ministers. The continuation of the system of communal electorates and the representation of special interests was recommended. So-called excluded areas occupied by the non-Burmese population were to be governed directly by the Governor. Commercial discrimination, the rights of civil servants, and the protection of minorities all received considerable attention from the com-

94

mittee.[41] In 1935 the Government of Burma Act was passed by Parliament.[42] Burma once again became a separate political entity on April 1, 1937, when the act became operative.

This new constitution of Burma largely abandoned the dyarchial system of divided executive and legislative authority introduced in 1923. The Governor, who had both legislative and executive functions, was the control mechanism in this scheme of developing self-rule in Burma. Responsible to the Secretary of State for India and Burma, the Governor was to operate within the framework of the Instrument of Instructions handed down from the India Office. By adjusting the instructions of the Governor to the political situation, the role of the ministers in the government could be expanded by increasing their responsibility to act in the name of the Governor. Thus the Governor was directed to select his ministers in consultation with the person most likely to command a stable majority in the legislature from among those members most likely to have the confidence of the legislature and to be guided by the advice of his ministers unless inconsistent with his responsibilities under the act.[43]

The Governor exercised sole control of certain reserved subjects: defense, external affairs,

Anglican ecclesiastical affairs, monetary policy, and the administration of the "excluded areas" largely inhabited by non-Burmese peoples. To assist him in this function the Governor could appoint three counsellors.

The Governor had special responsibilities with concomitant powers to protect certain basic interests of the British government and commercial interests in Burma. He was charged with the maintenance of internal peace, financial stability and credit, and the protection of minorities, the public services, and British and Indian commerce from discrimination. The Governor was authorized to "assume to himself all or any of the powers vested in or exercisable by anybody or authority in Burma at any time he should decide that a situation had arisen which precluded the normal operation of the government."[44]

A Council of Ministers was established to "aid and advise the Governor" in matters other than those reserved to the Governor or for which he had special responsibility. Subject to the limitations imposed by the Instrument of Instructions, the ministers, limited to ten, were chosen and held office at the pleasure of the Governor. In practice, however, the ministers "enjoyed the powers and privileges which were invested in the Cabinet of a self-governing Dominion."[45]

The upper house of the bicameral legislature,
the Senate, consisted of thirty-six members,
eighteen of whom were chosen by the Governor and
eighteen by the House of Representatives. Membership in the Senate was restricted to British subjects over thirty-five who were able to meet a
high property qualification or who had held high
public office. The House of Representatives was
elected and apportioned as follows:

General Constituencies 92
Reserved for:
Karens 12
Indians 8
Anglo-Burmese 2
Europeans 3
Commerce and Industry 11
Rangoon University 1
Indian Labor 2
Non-Indian Labor 1

While the ministers, counsellors, and advocate
general had the right to address either house, the
official bloc of votes was eliminated. The legislature was empowered to make the law of the land.
The Governor was vested with power to veto legislative acts or to withhold approval pending con-

97

sultation with the London government. Furthermore, the Secretary of State for Burma could veto any act approved by the Governor by appropriate action within one year.

Broad legislative powers were vested in the Governor. In excluded areas he enjoyed the sole right of legislation. During legislative recesses the Governor could promulgate emergency ordinances. The refusal of the legislature to allocate funds for matters in which the Governor had special respon- sibilities could be countered by an authorization for expenditures by the Governor. Finally the Governor had the power to enact laws which were not subject to any subsequent legislative act. The resevoir of power available to the Governor made the success of the program for the development of self-rule in Burma rest heavily on the discretion of this key official and on the confidence he could command from the Burmese community. Cady has stated, "The constitution of 1935 was thus in no sense a radical instrument. . . . It could and did provide valuable experience in parliamentary prac- tice and an opportunity, hitherto denied, to come to grips with agrarian problems."[46]

98

CHAPTER 5

THE DEVELOPMENT OF BURMESE ADMINISTRATORS

The "increasing association of Indians in every
branch of the administration" was set forth in
the Montagu declaration of 1917 as a cardinal
principle of British policy in India. $\lceil$ By such a
process of "Indianization," a gradual turnover in
the operation of the governmental machinery could
be effected while the Indians were receiving tutelage in self-administration. $\rceil$ The gradual infusion
of Indians into the government was conceived of as
a "bridge" to popular rule, which could be gradually
extended, presumably until the passage from colonial
administration to responsible government was completed.[1] It was necessary to implement this policy
on two levels in order to promote the growth of
responsible government in Burma. The Burmese would
have to receive increasingly wider opportunities to
exercise executive and legislative powers which
would associate them with the decision-making process in the government of Burma. This was essentially a task to be carried out through appropriate
adjustments in political institutions. To enable
Burmese to gain experience in the whole gamut of

governmental activity, it was necessary to bring an increasing number into the wider field of public services. This was the function of the "Burmanization" process, which sought to introduce more Burmese into the public services and employ more Burmese in responsible posts.[2] A Burmese minister dependent for the implementation of his policies upon high British civil servants responsible only to the Secretary of State in London was a political anomaly which had to be rectified before any consistent progress toward responsible government could be achieved.[3] The Burmese nationalists, while centering their demands on institutional reforms, also pressed for increased opportunities in the public services and for better educational facilities to prepare Burmese for such positions.

The public services in India in 1917 consisted of the subordinate, provincial, and superior services. The subordinate services which provided the bulk of the minor civil service officials engaged in the administration of the districts, subdistricts, and townships of Burma were largely staffed by Burmese. Above them were civil servants in the provincial and all-India superior services. In 1913, of the approximately 255 officials in Burma holding civil service appointments that paid from 200-300 rupees per month, 87, or about one-third, were

100

Buddhists.[4] In the middle grades (officials
earning Rs. 500-600 per month) only 32 of 186, or
about 17 percent, were Buddhists. The evidence presented to the Royal Commission on the Indian Public
Services indicated that these lower salaries did
not always attract the best candidates for subordinate positions.[5] Using salary as a rough in-
dication of the importance of subordinate civil
service positions, in 1913 the Burmese held only
minor posts usually concerned with local matters in
rural areas.

The provincial civil service, recruited by the
direct appointment of Burma residents or by promotion from the subordinate civil service, was considered to be the most important of the public
services for Burmanization, since the positions
entailed more responsibility than the subordinate
civil service. In 1913, Buddhists held 57 of the
132 posts in the Burma Provincial Service executive
branch rating a salary of 200 rupees or more. The
judicial branch of the provincial service was almost exclusively Buddhist (that is, Burmese).
Although confined in the main to the less important
positions, the Burmese did occupy roughly one-half
the posts in the provincial civil service in 1913.
An effective policy of associating Burmese in the
government meant increasing the importance of the

positions open to Burmese as well as the number of positions. Furthermore few Burmese served in the functional, nonprovincial All-India Services, such as the Forest Service. Since there were no Burmese in the Indian Civil Service (ICS) in 1913, a consistent policy would require the nomination of Burmese to this branch, or the reclassification of ICS positions as provincial civil positions and the appointment of Burmese to such posts.

In the mid-nineteenth century about three-quarters of the police force in British Burma had been recruited from Burmese and other indigenous races. Gradually, however, Indians had displaced the Burmese as the major ethnic component of the police in Burma until only the prevention and detection sections were staffed by Burmese in 1881.[6] The higher officers of the police force were all Europeans.

Prior to the initiation of the reform movement in 1917, Burmese held no important posts in the administration. The recruitment of Burmese for subordinate positions was largely a matter of administrative convenience. A policy of "Burmanization" of the public services had to widen the scope of functions performed by Burmese and introduce opportunities for assuming responsibility in order effectively to prepare Burma for self-rule

102

despite inadequacies in training and experience among the Burmese.

The presence of British and Indian officials in the higher posts of the public services in Burma was a constant spur to Burmese nationalism. Frequent clashes occurred in the Legislative Council over the composition and functioning of the civil services. Burmanization was the key issue, but the nationalists were likewise concerned with the problems of administrative retrenchment in positions occupied by Europeans and in checking the spread of bribery and corruption among government officials.[7]

One of the most significant resolutions introduced in the Legislative Council proposed that all the civil services in Burma be made exclusively provincial, thus excluding nondomiciled persons from eligibility. This motion was closely tied to the whole complex question of separation from India. The government maintained a neutral position and the motion was carried, but never implemented, until separation was effected.[8]

Burmanization did not bulk large in the nationalist demands at the various reform inquiries between 1917 and 1937, when other political issues were more prominent. Nevertheless, responsible Burmese leaders realized the need for a well-trained

bureaucracy to staff the machinery for self-government as well as the strength of Burmanization as
a rallying cry against the established regime.

The implementation of the policy of bringing the
Burmese into the upper levels of government proceeded slowly. Burmanization was approached
cautiously by British administrators who desired
to keep a firm hold on the decision-making power
within the government. The lack of Burmese personnel who could meet British standards for the
superior civil service was a real limitation. Not
until 1923 did a Burmese successfully pass the
rigorous examinations for the Indian Civil Service,
which staffed the superior posts in the administration. Four Burmese had previously entered this
select body by appointment. The Royal Commission
on the Superior Civil Service in India, sitting
in 1924, found that "it must be some years before
an adequate supply of qualified Burmans can be
available to man the Public Services."[9]

Recruitment for the Indian Civil Service was
conducted by methods designed primarily to select
likely candidates with a European university education. The bulk of the recruits were selected
by competitive examinations held in London, although
examinations were also held in India. Other members of the Indian Civil Service were directly

104

nominated in India along with special appointments made from members of the bar. Experienced civil servants were promoted from the provincial civil services. Until 1920 military officers were selected to occupy numerous important positions in the Burma administration.[10] At that time the policy was established of appointing successful Indian candidates to service outside of Burma and similarly of posting Burmese who passed the examinations only in their home province. The plan for the Indian Civil Service anticipated that 33 percent of the members of this body should be Indians, with a 1-1/2 percent increment per annum up to 48 percent.[11] Since Burmese were "Indians" by statute, they would have to compete for a portion of this quota. The Royal Commission on the Superior Civil Services did recommend that the services be recruited on a provincial basis but also recommended that the governments of India and Burma adjust this general policy to "local conditions."[12]

While opportunities for Burmese in the superior services were limited both by policy and high recruitment standards, there was a large number of posts in the subordinate and the provincial services which were best filled by the Burmese. The clerks in central government offices were chiefly Indians, but on the district level it was more often the Burmese who filled these positions.

The Burmese became more numerous in certain of the functional All-India Services organized on non-provincial lines. The minor posts in the Forest Service and in the Telegraph and Post Services drew an increasing number of Burmese.[13] However, other All-India Services such as the Medical Service remained largely European and Indian.[14]

There are no statistics which permit a close comparison of the extent to which Burmese had been associated in the government of their country during the period between World War I and World War II. In response to written questions in Commons, the British government stated on February 29, 1932, "The following figures show approximately the number of Europeans, Indians, and Burmans employed in the Civil Services of Burma, excluding the subordinate services: Europeans, 925; Burmans, 680; Indians, 237."[15]

The percentage of persons from Burma in the lower civil service positions roughly doubled between 1913 and 1932 but did not increase proportionately in the higher ranks of the civil service, where greater responsibility rested.

The process of bringing Burmese into more of the positions of responsibility in the government of their country was complicated by an involved

106

series of local conditions and British policy considerations. Education and experience were the two
qualifications which placed the most serious limitations on the appointment of Burmese to the
higher civil service posts. While education on
the lower levels resulted in Burma having one of
the highest literacy rates in Asia, there were few
Burmese who had received the higher education which
would prepare them for the more responsible positions in the administration. In particular, a very
limited number of Burmese had received an advanced,
European education or had even attended Indian
universities which accounted in part for the failure
of Burmese to qualify for the superior posts
staffed by the Indian Civil Service. The University
of Rangoon was not established until 1920. Technical education in Burma was almost nonexistent.
Lack of opportunity was allegedly accompanied by
an absence of interest in the professional careers
by Burmese in any significant numbers.[16]

Although many of the Burmese appointed to the
provincial civil service had risen from the lower
ranks of the subordinate service, there was a reluctance to entrust Burmese of limited experience
with the higher posts of the provincial services
or the Indian Civil Service. The British administrator maintained that "the country has been handi-

capped by the lack of men with experience in administration which can only be learned by serving an
apprenticeship in subordinate positions . . . ."[17]
However, apprenticeships in minor posts were
usually long and often consumed the better part of
the time an individual spent in service. Furthermore, long experience in a subordinate position was
no assurance that the person concerned was receiving
appropriate training for a more responsible post
on a higher level. The qualifications of the Burmese with limited education sometimes precluded
a rise to the top positions requiring specialized
training. Nevertheless, British administrators
generally considered promotion based on experience
in the lower ranks as the most reliable method of
securing competent Burmese for service in the
higher positions.[18]

Another special consideration in the Burmanization of the civil service was the Indian problem.
Indians, many of whom were educated and experienced
in British administrative practices, had been an
important element in the civil service in Burma
since the inception of British rule. The presence
of a non-Burmese in the government was both a goad
to the national pride of the Burmese and a barrier
to the Burmanization of the civil services. The
technical positions such as medicine, forestry, and

transportation were the special bailiwick of the
Indians and Anglo-Burmese. The Montagu-Chelmsford
Report in 1917 recognized that increasingly associating Indians in the administration of Burma
would only mean replacing one alien bureaucracy
with another.[19] The Indians, who were usually
better qualified for the higher positions, pro-
tested any efforts to exclude them from the services
in Burma, insisting that appointment be made solely
on the basis of merit. Of the 18,117 persons employed in the general service of the governments
of India and Burma in Burma (1931), 4,768 were Indians born outside of Burma.[20] Gradually, with the
increase in education and experience among the Burmese, and especially after the separation from India and related political acts, the importance of
the Indian in the civil services in Burma dimin-
ished.

The Indian Civil Service was among the highest
paid in the world and drew capable careerists, who
took a special pride in their service. Many of
these men were reluctant to see the higher posts
in the public services taken over by untried Burmese. The Royal Commission on the Superior Civil
Services recommended a gradual process of "Indianization" of the Indian Civil Service until the
number of Europeans and Indians was about equal in

1939. The British administrators were unwilling
to accelerate this slow pace, and the goal was not
yet achieved in 1939. Furthermore, the Governor
was charged with special responsibilities in pro-
tecting the rights of the public services. The
presence of an entrenched European group in the
upper posts of the civil service could only serve
to impede the process of Burmanization.

Corruption within the civil service was one
further barrier to rapid Burmanization. Under the
Burmese kings, Burmese officials had received no
salary but had taken a portion of the revenue they
collected. This was the accepted process, and only
with the advent of British rule was the concept
of a salaried, disciplined civil service introduced.
Prior to the 1923 reforms, little attention was
given to the conduct of public officials. With the
increase in political awareness in Burma, the corruption in the public services became a target for
nationalist criticism. In the 1927-1928 session
of the Legislative Council, a motion on bribery and
corruption introduced by a leader of the Home Rule
Party led to a walkout staged by the opposition
parties.[21] With the growth of ministerial responsibility, there were inevitably increased opportunities for patronage and temptations of bribery
and corruption.

110

Not until the Burmese nationalists assumed a greater role in the government under the 1937 reformed constitution was a systematic investigation made of bribery and corruption in the civil services. The investigating committee concluded that only 30 percent of the general and judicial branches of the provincial and subordinate services was honest. The police were of even more doubtful integrity, since about two-thirds of the inspectors were corrupt. The consensus of the testimony was that the Excise Department was almost universally corrupt. A similar pattern of behavior was general in most of the branches of the civil service. This included all personnel, many of whom, of course, were not Burmese.

Corruption appears to have been less wide-spread in such branches of the government as the Irrigation Department, where Burmese officials were numerous and the function of the department was geared to the needs of the people in a direct and understandable manner. The multiplication of public services in ways which appeared to increase the burden of the ordinary citizen in turn increased the propensity for, and the likelihood of, bribery and corruption. In the eyes of one experienced British official generally sympathetic to the Burmese nationalists, "The main cause of corruption in the

services was the cleavage between law and custom
and the contradiction between administrative policy
and public sentiment."[22] While corruption in the
administration might deter a policy of Burmanization
as preparation of self-rule, the vigorous attitude
for reform espoused by the Burmese nationalists indicated that the necessary adjustments to public
needs and customs could serve to reduce the serious-
ness of this problem.

The limitations placed on Burmanization of the
civil services by the lack of education and experience, by the prevalence of Indians and Europeans,
and by corruption were all related to a basic consideration in British policy: administrative
efficiency. Here again the program of increasing
the role of the Burmese in the government as a
step in preparation for self-rule had to be adapted
to meet the needs of maintaining a reasonably
effective administration. For this reason Burma
faced self-rule with inadequately trained personnel
to staff the administration.

CHAPTER 6

THE DEVELOPMENT OF A VIABLE SOCIAL STRUCTURE

Throughout the period of Burma's emergence from a
colonial status Burmese nationalists were concerned
with the role of minorities in Burma's social stru-
ture and eradicating one conspicuous hallmark of
colonialism--the concentration of political and
economic power in the hands of nonindigenous minorities. The British and Indian administrators and
the commercial class constituted the upper strata
of a fundamentally plural society. The development
of a viable independent state in Burma, in the eyes
of some nationalists, demanded a closing of the
breach created by the plural society through the
repatriation or assimilation of these nonindigenous
minorities. Controversies arising out of demands
for separation from India, political representation
for minorities, and discrimination were more than
random expressions of Burmese nationalism, being
directly related to the consolidation of the plural
society of colonial Burma into a politically unified society of a modern nation-state.

The divergences among the indigenous people of
Burma were not unsurmountable barriers to the de-

velopment of a unitary state in Burma. The Burmese were by far the largest ethnic group. These
people were mainly farmers living in the river
valleys and plains. The horseshoe of mountains and
plains rimming Burma on all its land frontiers was
inhabited by other indigenous groups having greatly
varying levels of cultural and political development.
The Talaings (Mons), who had contended with the Burmese for centuries for control of Burma, were con-
clusively defeated in the middle of the eighteenth
century. Gradually the Talaings were absorbed by
the Burmese until they lost their identity as a
minority after the establishment of British rule.
Although the political and cultural assimilation
of the Talaings was achieved through forceful methods, it demonstrated that the Burmese society was
capable of gradually assimilating at least some of
the indigenous minority groups.[1]

The relations of the Karen minority of 1,367,673
(1930) with the Burmese presented the most serious
barriers to workable relationships among the indigenous peoples of Burma. One body of Karens occupied Karenni, a state separate from British India
but under the administration of the Burma government. Another sizable group was scattered among
the Burmese in the delta area. Antagonism between
the Burmese and Karens was compounded by the advent
114

of Western institutions. The Karens developed a loyalty to the British administration. They were recruited to put down persistent Burmese resistance to British rule and thereafter were the core of military forces raised in Burma. The Sgaw, one of the two major groups of Karens, came under the influence of Christian missionaries, which served to widen their differences with the Burmese. To a large extent "missionaries bear the responsibility for slowing up the process of 'Burmanization' of this important minority group."[2] The Pwo Karens, less exposed to Christian influence, tended to be absorbed and nominally accepted Buddhism. Karen nationalist leaders from 1917 on pressed demands for separate political representation in the legislature but many British officials, though sympathetic to the Karens, felt that Karen interests were not so distinct from those of the Burmese that special representation would be required. However, such representation was granted in 1923.

The 1,037,046 (1930) Shans comprised the third most numerous ethnic group in Burma. The political status of these people presented a special case since they were located almost exclusively in the Shan States administered by local chiefs (<u>sawbwas</u>) under the guidance of British officials. The Shan States were reserved to the Governor for adminis-

tration so that Burmese ministers gained no experience in handling Shan affairs. However, the
Buddhist Shans and Burmese had no major differences,
and Burmese nationalists did not actively contest
the Shan claim to autonomy within any self-governing
state which might be established in Burma.

The numerous other indigenous peoples of Burma
had only very basic forms of social and political
organization and displayed no interest in the movement for self-rule in Burma. The Burmese and the
animistic Kachins gradually pushing into Burma from
the north developed animosities, but the Chins of
the western hill areas accepted Buddhism to some
extent and were in the process of assimilation or
acculturation. Even after the reforms of 1923 and
1935 these tribal peoples were excluded from the
regular administration, and, hence, Burmese gained
no first-hand experience in dealing with these
hill peoples who presumably would be incorporated
in a self-governing Burma.

Buddhism and spirit worship were common religious ties shared by the major groups in Burma.
Most of the people of Burma were peasants living in
rural villages. Furthermore, they shared a common
element in their historical background under the
kings of Burma. Despite Karen demands for special
representation in the legislature, Shan insistence

116

upon autonomy and the relative isolation of other
hill peoples, the indigenous population of Burma at
the time seemed to be sufficiently homogenous to
permit the establishment of a modern nation-state.[3]

The major problems in development of a cohesive
nation-state in Burma, as perceived by the Burmese
nationalists in the 1920s, proceeded from the concentration of economic and political power in the
hands of nonindigenous minorities, particularly the
Indians and Europeans (British). The 1,100,000
Indians in Burma were the special target of Burmese
nationalists.[4] The British employed in administration of the government and business were remote
from the personal experience of the Burmese peasant
and laborer. The Indian moneylender, landowner,
agricultural laborer, and coolie were much closer
to the peasants of Lower Burma and much more
directly associated with their everyday problems.

To many Burmese tenant farmers, debtors, and
laborers the Indians were either absentee landlords,
usurious moneylenders, or undercutting low wage
laborers. The leaders of the Indian minority ada-
mantly contested separation from India while generally supporting the colonial government in the local
legislature.

The commercialization of rice culture in the
lower Irrawaddy basin stimulated the immigration of

Indian agricultural and rice-mill labor to Burma. The development of new agricultural areas required capital which was provided by Indian investors and moneylenders. Other demands for cheap labor accompanying the economic development of Burma stimulated the flow of Indians. Indian immigration reached a peak of 428,343 persons during the 1928 harvest year.[5] Most Indian laborers came to Burma for a brief three- to five-year period. Though the Indian Statutory Commission ventured the opinion that "the steady excess of Indian immigrants over Indian emigrants may be a measure rather of economic development than of Indian penetration of Burma," the Burmese increasingly regarded the Indians as competitors in the labor market or exploiters of the local peasants.[6] The Burmese nationalists anticipated controlling immigration after gaining political power, while the Indian interests sought to secure safeguards against anticipated discrimination even after Burma was separated.

During the nineteenth century there had been a good possibility of the Indian minority becoming assimilated through intermarriage and through the gradual elimination of economic and social distinctions. However, the rise of nationalism in India and then in Burma, along with mounting agrarian difficulties of peasants in Burma involving Indian

118

landlords, checked the trend toward assimilation.[7]

Village raids, clashes in the paddy fields, and riots in Rangoon and other centers of Indian population marked the growing hostility of the aroused Burmese toward the Indian minority. A dispute over ownership of some paddy land in 1920, which led to a rice-field fight between some thirty Indians and forty Burmese, typified the growing Burmese antagonism toward the Indian minority.[8]

The economic depression of the early 1930s threw urban Burmese into competition with Indians as dock laborers; work which the Burmese heretofore had avoided. When Indian dock laborers in Rangoon struck for higher wages in 1930, they were replaced by Burmese. Attempts to displace the Burmese when the strike was settled in May provoked open fighting requiring the use of troops to restore order. According to the official report about a hundred persons were killed and a thousand injured, almost exclusively Indians. Though Burmese dock labor was considered unskilled and more expensive than Indian labor, the conciliation board which settled the strike awarded 50 percent of the work to the Burmese laborers.[9]

The Rangoon riots of May, 1930, were a preview of more violent and widespread attacks on Indians, which accompanied the nationalist rebellion launched in December, 1930. Though the uprising led by Saya San was initially directed against the government, the collapse of law and order in widespread rural areas permitted the Burmese villagers to give vent to their antagonism against the Indians. Indians in rural areas fled to Rangoon, but attacks persisted and became so serious that emigration from Burma surpassed immigration until order was restored. The Burmese nationalist organization Dobama called upon the Burmese to drive the Indians out of the country.[10] The extensive attacks on Indians, which occurred in rural areas, highlighted the antagonism between the Burmese peasants and the Indians, who symbolized alien economic domination, absentee landlordism, and rural indebtedness.

The Chinese minority of 193,594 (1930) presented no obstacles to the development of a homogenous nation-state in Burma. Mainly shopkeepers and artisans, the Chinese in Burma were not as economically embroiled with the local population as were the Indians and did not generate similar antagonisms. The principal exceptions were the Chinese shopkeepers who extended credit at usurous terms. In January, 1931, during the turmoil of the rebellion, riots between Burmese and Chinese flared up in Rangoon causing fourteen deaths and a Chinese exodus from Rangoon.[11] Generally, however, there was

120

greater Burmese affinity with the Chinese than with the Indians.[12]

The Chinese were not British subjects and took little part in local politics. The Chinese Chamber of Commerce member of the Legislative Council usually supported the government. The Chinese minority, while maintaining its cultural identity, made satisfactory adjustments with the Burmese society. Barring large increments in Chinese immigration to Burma which might provoke the concern of Burmese nationalists, the Chinese minority could be politically integrated within a self-governing Burma.

A special case was presented by the Anglo-Burmese, who shunned the indigenous peoples and yet were not fully accepted by the European community. This group attempted to protect its position by legal safeguards and special representation in the legislature. While not absorbed into the Burmese social pattern, the Anglo-Burmese seemed capable of finding their place and making important contributions in a self-governing Burma.[13]

The British in Burma were essentially a concomitant of British rule and could not be expected to maintain their connections with Burma for any long period after the people of Burma assumed responsibility for the government of the country.

Hence the problem of a British minority in any future independent state of Burma was insignificant, although British economic interests in Burma would probably persist after the transfer of political power.

The British policy toward minorities in Burma was continually suspect by Burmese nationalists who viewed special measures for minorities as part of a plan of "divide and rule." British administrators in Burma usually met minority problems on an ad hoc basis without specifically relating them to either the preservation of British power or of promoting a unified society as a part of the policy of developing self-rule in Burma. The special status of the European minority was of course given political recognition, but the relations of the Burmese to the Indians, Karens, and Shans had to be considered not only within the context of the situation at the time, but also with a view to their possible role in a self-governing Burma. In general, the treatment of minorities was conceived of within the framework of the overall policy of promoting economic development and administrative efficiency. The promotion of Indian immigration to Burma, the political representation of economic interests, and the advocacy of separation from India by the Burma government all were related to the policy of economic development. Administrative convenience in part dictated the British policy toward minorities in the army and civil services in Burma, the administration of the frontier areas, and certain aspects of political representation of minorities. A program of fostering political cohesion between the Burmese and the minorities was not an integral part of the British policy of developing self-rule in Burma.

The political representation of minorities in the Burma Legislative Council, an institutional manifestation of Burma's pluralistic society, was initiated in 1923. The principle of communal representation aimed at securing political representation for groups that would not ordinarily seat members due to their numerical weaknesses. In 1909 special representation had been given to the Burma Chamber of Commerce and the Rangoon Trades Association. While communal representation was ostensibly devised to protect the interest of minorities, it often proved to be a means of representation for specific economic interests.[14] Minorities entitled to communal representation elected a specified number of candidates from their group to occupy seats in the Legislative Council. As was often the case with political institutions in Burma, the system of communal representation was

123

transferred from India. Burmese nationalists opposed this type of constituency, again raising the cry of "divide and rule,"[15] and contesting the existence of special minority interests, which could be differentiated from the general interests of the people of Burma generally. The Burma Reforms Committee admitted that communal representation was theoretically undesirable and attempted to modify this scheme by proposing reserved seats for Indians and Karens in certain plural member constituencies. This would have made the Indian or Karen occupants of the special seats responsible to the general constituency that elected them. This provoked a struggle between the advocates and opponents of communal representation in which the former gained the upper hand. The communal seats in the 1923 Legislative Council were allocated as follows:

Indian (Urban)	8
Karen	5
Anglo-Indian	1
European	1

There were also the members elected by special interests:

Burma Chamber of Commerce	2
Burmese Chamber of Commerce	1
Indian Chamber of Commerce	1
Chinese Chamber of Commerce	1
Rangoon Trades Association	1
Rangoon University	1

Communal representation in the Legislative Council
institutionalized and helped perpetuate the dif-
ferentiation of group interests along communal
lines. Non-European minorities remained politically apart from the Burmese striving for self-rule
except when a specific interest of the minority
was at stake. This attitude had its counterpart
in a growing exclusiveness among the Burmese who
accepted the minorities as political associates
on an ad hoc basis only, as during the separation
controversy. The government generally depended
on a conglomeration of representatives of minority
and special interests to push its program through
the Legislative Council in the face of opposition
of Burmese nationalists. The Governor had adequate powers to extend protection to the minorities, and in case of discriminatory legislation,
the Governor-General in New Delhi had the authority to reject such bills as he did the Sea Pas-
sengers Tax Bill (1925) upon protest by the In-

dians in Burma.[16]

The investigations of constitutional reform which led to the Government of Burma Act, 1935, were replete with arguments for increasing the number of minorities granted communal representation as well as increasing the number of seats held by those already entitled to representation. Muslims and Christians, a landowners association, and special segments of the Indian community all bid for separate representation in the legislature. The Secretary of State for India favored the retention of the communal seats for Europeans, Indians, Anglo-Indians, and Karens, although opposing its extension to other groups, particularly on a religious basis.[17]

The Burmese delegates to the Round Table Conference and witnesses before the commissions of inquiry either denied the existence of separate minority interests or advocated other means of safeguarding minority rights.[18]

Organized Indian interests in Burma were primarily concerned with maintaining the province's ties with India. However, they also pushed for "better and more adequate" representation in the legislature, claiming one-fifth of the seats.[19] Two seats in the legislature were claimed by the Chinese. The Karens insisted that communal representation alone prevented them from being virtually excluded from the Legislative Council, only one Karen being elected from a general constituency. The Karen elders asked that their people be given eleven seats.[20] The Anglo-Indians and Domiciled European Association asked for four representatives to the Legislative Council, while another British organization asserted that the minority represen- tatives should comprise 30 percent of the lower house.[21] If all the claims of the minorities for seats in the lower house had been granted, they would have held 49 percent of the seats in the legislature.[22]

	Elected Legis- lative Council Seats 1923	Seats Claimed 1930	Seats Granted in the House of Representatives Government of Burma Act 1935
General Constituencies	58		92
Indian (Urban)	8	15-16	8
Karen	5	12	12
European	1	12-13	3

	Legislative Council Seats 1923	Seats Claimed 1930	Seats Granted in the House of Representatives Government of Burma Act 1935
Anglo-Indian (Anglo-Burmese)	1	3	2
Burma Chamber of Commerce	2	6	5
Burmese Chamber of Commerce	1		1
Indian Chamber of Commerce	1		2
Chinese Chamber of Commerce	1	2	1
Rangoon Trades Association	1	1	1
Wattukotlais Chettyars' Association			1
Non-Indian Labor			1
Indian Labor			2
Rangoon University	1		1

The communal system, introduced in 1923 and strengthened in 1935, impeded the development of effective linkages between the interests of minority groups and those of the essentially homogenous majority of Burma.

The next stage of the problem of developing national unity was that of Burma's political identity with relation to India. A self-governing

128

Burma was necessarily premised on eventual separation from India and emergence from the status of
a province to that of separate political entity.
The necessity for separation from India was strengthened as India approached self-rule, because it was
not possible for Burmese nationalists to conceive
of Burma as a permanent part of an independent
India.[23]

Burma, a Buddhist kingdom with its own traditions and ethos, had been incorporated into the
Indian Empire peopled predominately by Hindus and
Muslims. Administrative convenience dictated that
Burma be governed as a province of India.[24] Through
this political association grew up a multitude of
ties that immensely complicated the problem of
severing Burma's connection with India a century
later. Deeper than these largely administrative
difficulties was the uneasy suspicion with which
Burmese nationalists regarded British efforts to
promote separation, fearing that Burma would be
denied the reforms granted to India.

As a province of India, Burma was entitled to
representation in the Indian Legislative Assembly
and Council of State meeting in New Delhi. However,
the political and geographic remoteness of Burma
from the capital of India precluded effective participation of representatives from Burma in Indian

legislative bodies. Difficulty was experienced in securing representatives, and those who did serve were of no importance in the Indian legislature. The nonofficial representatives to the Legislative Assembly from Burma complained: "Burma is a Province in which nobody in this House is taking any special interest, and of which nobody has got any special knowledge. . . ."[25] The only occasion when Burma received attention in the legislature at New Delhi was when Indian interests in Burma were involved. Burma's membership in these bodies was a symbol of her provincial status, which would be terminated when Burma regained its separate status.

The Burmese in the provincial government gained no experience in dealing with subjects handled from New Delhi, particularly in foreign affairs and defense policy. This would be the case so long as Burma remained a part of India.

Hostility toward the Indians in Burma was a weighty factor in the separation controversy. The mounting Burmese animosity toward Indians gave rise to demands for separation, which would presumably enable barriers to be raised to block large-scale Indian immigration to Burma. The Burmese apprehensions regarding the ultimate effect of unlimited Indian immigration were made known to Montagu during his investigation of Indian constitu-

130

tional reform.[26] For their part, the Indians were fearful of immigration restrictions if Burma were cast loose from India, and they tried to thwart separation or, failing that, to secure safeguards if Burma were separated. Economic difficulties of the Burmese fortified growing sentiment for deterring Indian immigration to Burma. Under Section 138 of the Government of Burma Act (1935) and the implementing Government of Burma (Immigration) Order, 1937, immigration into Burma from India was free from any restrictions except those already in force prior to separation for three years after separation.[27] The intricate web of Indo-Burmese relations precluded a summary barring of Indian immigration to Burma, even after separation, despite Burmese desires to rid themselves of economic problems attributed to the Indians by cutting off immigration. Strong economic motives for separation also sprung from the desire of business interests in Burma, primarily British, to establish a separate tariff schedule and tax system for Burma.[28]

A factor more directly related to the establishment of Burma as a separate state was the military relationship of the province to the rest of India. The Montagu-Chelmsford Report advanced the opinion that military reasons dictated that Burma remain a part of India.[29] During the nineteenth

131

century, the Burma government had experimented with recruiting Tailangs, Arakanese, Karens, and Shans for the army, primarily to complete the conquest of Burma. The British considered the Burmese unsuited for military service and more expensive to maintain as soldiers than if other ethnic groups were recruited. Indians provided the bulk of the British forces in Burma while the Karens became the most important indigenous element in the armed forces.[30] Burmese were recruited to serve in Mesopotamia, Palestine, and France during World War I, but after the emergency the use of Burmese in the armed forces lapsed. Governor Craddock attached "the greatest importance to the establishment of a military tradition among the indigenous races of Burma and in the increasing employment of men of these races both in the regular army and in the irregular forces maintained on the Frontier."[31] However, Army Headquarters in India, concerned with retrenchment, ceased recruiting Burmese for the regular infantry and utilized only Karens, Kachins, and Chins from among the indigenous peoples. The Burma government demurred from this decision on political grounds, but the Burmese were excluded from the Indian Army until 1929.[32] Indians advanced the defense problem as an argument against separation, but in 1929 the Commander-in-Chief of the Indian

132

Army conceded that unified control for the defense
of India and Burma was not essential.[33] The Indian
Statutory Commission was impressed with the fact
that Burma's contribution toward defense was not
commensurate with the actual expenditures for troops
in Burma.[34] The Burmese who favored separation felt
that the Imperial defense system would provide
adequate protection for the future state of Burma.
A real concern of the nationalists was the failure
of the Burmese to acquire adequate training for
national defense or to establish a real Burma national military force.[35] A memorandum by the more
moderate Burmese nationalists to the Joint Parliamentary Committee investigating Indian constitutional reform in 1933 proposed the establishment of
a military council for Burma to train appropriate
persons from Burma in military policy and also proposed that the new Burma legislature be permitted
to discuss military questions.[36]

As late as 1939 two years after separation, the
Burmese were only a minor component of the Burma
Army.[37]

Ethnic Group	Percent of the Population	Number in Army
Burmese	75.11	472
Karen	9.34	1448
Chin	2.38	868

133

Ethnic Group	Percent of the Population	Number in Army
Kachin	1.05	881
Others		
Native	2.38	168
Foreign	9.74	

Clearly the need to prepare Burma for self-rule and to give a sense of modern nationhood, by the development of an indigenous armed force in which the Burmese played an important role, had been neglected in the interest of other policy demands.

CHAPTER 7

THE RELATIONSHIP OF THE INDIVIDUAL TO THE GOVERNMENT

The effective operation of the representative political institutions that were evolving in Burma under
the guidance of the British administrators and policy
makers demanded greatly increased public interest
and participation in the political process. The experience of the people of Burma with the workings of
government prior to British rule was confined largely
to village situations.[1] Beginning in 1923, the majority of the adult males were called upon to interest themselves in district and provincial affairs
as well as developments in New Delhi and London relating to Burma and to elect representatives for
Circle Boards, the Legislative Council, and the Indian Legislature. The political lassitude of the
Burmese, decried in 1917 by the opponents of reform,
persisted ten years later despite the crescendo of
criticism by a comparatively small group of nationalists and occasional outbursts of nationalist activity by groups of Burmese.[2] A comprehensive
policy for developing self-rule in Burma would
necessarily seek to stimulate a broader public
interest and participation in the government.

Various techniques were available to bring the individual into a more direct relationship with his government: extending the franchise, nurturing the growth of public opinion, broadening the scope of the rights and duties of the individual, promoting education, and fostering local self-government. By such methods the political awareness of the population of Burma might have been stimulated and directed into channels that would enhance the growth of a government responsible to the electorate.

The people of Burma, who had had no experience with national elections, were granted virtual manhood suffrage under the 1923 reforms. The sudden opening of the political process to the voters of Burma did not lead to any marked increase in public interest in the government and seemed to justify the arguments of the opponents of reform who underscored the political lethargy of the general public.

The Burma government, faced with a difficult technical problem in establishing the basis for the franchise, supported proposals for a very broad electorate, principally for reasons of administrative convenience. Citizens reaching the age of eighteen were subject to certain general taxes: in Upper Burma the thathemada tax was levied on all household heads, and in Lower Burma the capitation tax was levied on males. As the individual's name

136

first appeared on the tax rolls at the age of
eighteen, it was simpler to establish the electoral
rolls from tax registrations than to set up a
separate list of voters.[3] The residents in municipalities who owned a minimum of property or paid a
basic rent were entitled to vote. Some of the British officials favored basing the franchise on payment of a land tax which, however, made voting eligibility difficult to determine. Others proposed a
literacy test.[4] The majority of the British members of the bureaucracy supported the wide franchise proposals though they regarded the move as a
"leap in the dark." The consensus of the British
civil service seemed to be that since so very few
citizens were prepared to exercise the franchise it
was just as reasonable to extend the ballot to a
large number of politically inexperienced persons
as it was to give the vote to a smaller number,
though equally inexperienced. In Meiktila District
11,000 persons would have qualified to vote under
the more narrow land revenue basis for the franchise compared with about 50,000 who paid the thathemada tax. The Deputy Commissioner of the district was of the opinion that the 50,000 were just
as capable or incapable of voting as were the
11,000, so that the broader franchise was just as
valid, because there were probably no more than

fifty politically conscious persons in the district.[5] The more earnest advocates of the wider
franchise saw such a move as a method of political
education and a deterent to agitation. The liberal
franchise grant of 1923 made one person in six in
Burma eligible to vote for the Legislative Council
and various local government bodies.

The Burmese public made a very limited response
to the opportunity to take a direct part in the
government of their country. In 1922, participation in the election was 6.92 percent; in 1925,
16.26 percent.[6]

While the indifference of the people of Burma
to their government was a major factor in the
limited use of the ballot, other factors accounted
in part for these conditions. The most obvious
was the boycott of the polls instituted by the
Burmese nationalists. When one group of nationalists decided to contest the 1925 election, there
was an increase in the number of voters participating. To the extent that the nationalist boycott was heeded, the small turnouts for elections
did not indicate indifference, but rather were a
negative expression of a very positive political
attitude.[7] The political apathy of many of the
rural population was associated with an unfamili-

138

arity with the democratic forms of political activity and a skepticism as to the real powers of the representative bodies. Technical problems of location of polling places, facilities for political campaigns, and dissemination of information further militated against a widespread participation in Burma's elections.[8] The effective use of the ballot to associate the individual with the governing process was further impeded by abuses of the franchise. The opponents of reform could point to cases of corruption in elections, personation, and mass voting by Indian laborers in Rangoon under their employers' direction.[9]

The failure of a liberal franchise to arouse the Burmese from their political somnolence was discouraging to the proponents of constitutional reform but there was no retracing of steps already taken. Slight rectifications might be made in the suffrage but it was politically unfeasible to contract the scope of the franchise. The Burmese nationalists concentrated their efforts for franchise reform to narrowing the scope of eligible voters by redefining citizenship so as to exclude nonindigenous persons without a long period of domicile in Burma.[10] Other proposals advocated the extension of the franchise to women and the raising of the age of eligibility for voting from eighteen to twenty-one.

However, the slight modifications in the franchise under the 1935 reforms followed closely the revisions suggested by the government of Burma. Payment of the capitation or _thathemada_ tax remained the basis of the franchise until 1937, when these two taxes were abolished. Since women as well as men were required to pay the _thathemada_ tax levied in Upper Burma, 86 percent of the female voters were residents of that section of Burma. Urban residents owning Rs. 200 of immovable property or occupying a house renting for Rs. 60 per annum were entitled to vote.[11]

The relations between the individual and the government under British rule were determined to a considerable extent by Western concepts of personal liberties. Under ordinary conditions the residents of Burma enjoyed a comparatively wide degree of freedom of the press and speech. There were no restrictions on freedom of religion.[12]

The Governor was given wide powers to maintain law and order in Burma, which enabled the government to set aside individual liberties in times of emergency. In addition, the Governor was given responsibilities under special acts designed to meet specific problems of internal security. One of the most notorious of these pieces of legis-

lation was the Anarchical Revolutionary Crimes Act
(Rowlatt) enacted by the Governor-General of India
in Council in 1919.[13] This act, passed upon conclusion of the investigation of the revolutionary
movement in India by the Rowlatt Commission, was
in force three years after the end of World War I.
Its purpose was to provide for the speedy trial
of offenses "in the interest of the public safety."
When, in the opinion of the local government, there
were reasonable grounds for believing that a person
was or had been involved in anarchical or revolutionary movements in areas in which the act was
made operative by the Governor-General, the local
(provincial) government had the power to direct the
individual to post a bond that he would not commit
or conspire to commit any of the specified offenses
and would remain in a designated area. The local
government was given enforcement powers to arrest
and search without warrant and confine a prisoner
under its own conditions up to fifteen days.

     The Anarchical and Revolutionary Crimes Act
was designed principally to meet conditions in India
and to supplement the wide powers given to the
Governor-General under the Defense of India Ordinances of 1915. Some of the powers of the Rowlatt
Act were extended beyond their three-year limit in
the Burma Habitual Offenders Restriction Act of

1919. The purpose of this law was to control the movements of so-called habitual offenders by either confining them to a certain village or area or by requiring them to report to proper authorities at stated times and places or both.[14] This was part of the network of controls, operating through the Criminal Investigation Department of the Burma Police, by which the government attempted to stem the increasing crime rate. The Burma Criminal Law (Amendment) Act, 1922, placed the burden upon the accused to prove that he had ownership of articles suspected to have been stolen in certain cases.[15]

Nevertheless, these acts which gave the government of Burma wide authority to restrict personal liberties failed to achieve their primary objective of checking crime in Burma. The Criminal Tribes Act, as revised in 1924, extended governmental powers. This law enabled the government to apply the restrictions of the Habitual Offenders Act to groups of individuals. Any tribe, gang, or class which the Burma government believed was addicted to the systematic commission of serious offenses might be declared a criminal tribe. The members of such "tribes" had to report at fixed intervals and to notify the government of any changes in residence. The government had the further power to establish industrial, agricultural, or refor-

142

matory settlements for criminal "tribes." Registered members of criminal "tribes" found under suspicious circumstances could be given up to three years imprisonment and fined. These circumstances included being caught about to commit or aid in a theft or robbery or "waiting for an opportunity" to commit these crimes.[16] This act was employed extensively by the government of Burma. Freedom of assembly was curtailed during the Burma Reform Committee's visit to Rangoon in December, 1921, under the Prevention of Seditious Meetings Act.[17] The press in Burma took on an increasingly nationalistic, antigovernment tone. The government had power to seize publications adjudged seditious, although during the 1920s, at least, confiscated materials were usually Indian nationalist tracts. Rigorous controls were exercised over firearms through a process of licensing dealers and owners. While the inhabitants of Burma were heirs to a variety of legal rights as a result of British rule, many of which were alien to their society, they found that during periods of internal insecurity, severe inroads were made into the rights of the individual, particularly with regard to the judicial process. This conditional aspect of personal liberties in Burma impaired the development of confidence in the government by the people of Burma,

and, in turn, impeded the overall policy for developing self-rule in Burma.

The body of rights and duties of the individual in Burma affected the relationship of the individual to the government to a considerable extent
only under such special circumstances as during a
legal proceeding or during an election. The British
policy makers interested in promoting the development of self-rule in Burma placed great emphasis
on the participation of the individual in local
self-government. The government of India recommended that there be complete popular control in local
bodies in Burma coupled with the largest possible
independence of outside control.[18] If the people
of Burma could learn to cope with the limited problems on the village and district level in which
they presumably had a more immediate interest, it
was felt that their political horizon could be
more effectively extended to the provincial government. Local self-government was considered as an
institution for training in responsible citizenship.[19] While the experience gained in participating in the affairs of a village or district was of
limited value in meeting problems of national
policy, the expansion of the area of participation
in local self-government might possibly have developed a greater interest in the political process
144

among the Burmese.[20]

The local government, which had operated under the Burmese kings, was displaced by a foreign legal system, which was primarily concerned with administrative efficiency and economic development. The reorganization of local government under British rule, particularly on the village level, disrupted traditional controls on antisocial forces without providing the machinery to check these forces.[21] The reestablishment of the organic ties between local government institutions and the needs of the villager would have contributed to restoring social stability and promoting rapport between the government and its people.

The Burma Rural Self-Government Act of 1921 established the framework for local government on the intermediary level between the village and central government. The Circle Boards consisted of representatives elected by a broad electorate in groups of village tracts. The Circle Boards in turn elected District Councils from among their number. The twenty-eight District Councils were responsible for local funds, for secondary roads, waterways, health services, and schools. These functions could in turn be delegated to the Circle Boards, bringing the control of these services closer to the individual citizen.

The Circle Boards ran into a series of difficulties which made them virtually inoperative.
The election boycott instituted by the nationalists
was extended to the voting for local government
bodies. In the first election of 1922, there were
2,738 groups of village tracts scheduled to elect
members to 287 Circle Boards. In 597 groups of village tracts there were no candidates, while in 776
groups there was no election contest.[22] The situation failed to improve in 1925 even though some of
the nationalist factions abandoned the boycott.

<u>Elections for Circle Boards</u>[23]

	Percent of village tracts in which required number of candidates not nominated	Percent of village tracts where there were contests	Percent of persons voting in contested groups
1922	22.6	28.3	24.36
1925	21.0	23.8	24.83

Another difficulty was that village headmen
(<u>thugyis</u>) were among the few persons on the village
level with enough political experience or interest
to serve on Circle Boards. Burmese nationalists
considered the <u>thugyis</u> as officials rather than
representatives of the people and maintained that
the <u>thugyis</u> on the Circle Boards would only serve
to perpetuate the bureaucratic method of village

146

administration. However, the Burma Rural Self-
Government Bill provided that thugyis elected to
the Circle Boards could be seated if they resigned
their village position.[24] The third major reason
for the failure of the Circle Boards as an instrument of local self-government was the neglect of
the District Councils to delegate functions to
their parent bodies.[25] Aside from electing members
to the District Councils, the Circle Boards had no
reason for existence. The little interest that did
exist in the boards soon died, and the boards re-
peatedly failed to hold the prescribed number of
meetings.[26]

The District Councils, though off to a more
hopeful start than the Circle Boards, soon waned
through the lack of public interest from below and
an excess of supervision from above. Branded as
"dyarchic councils" because of their association in
the public mind with the system of dyarchy introduced in the central government about the same time,
the District Councils labored under the difficulties of incomplete membership, inadequate revenues,
and nationalist opposition.[27] The councils were
devised with the expectation that they would more
closely associate the expenditure of funds with the
local needs, but a reluctance to allocate funds for
education and health purposes with which the major-

147

ity of Burmese were unfamiliar soon developed.
Whatever funds were available were inexpertly
handled and the District Council accounts usually
failed to measure up to the standards applied by
the Burma government.[28]

The shortage of candidates in the first elections for the Circle Boards and the prospect that
the election would fail to provide full membership
made the prospects for these new local government
bodies so uncertain that the Rural Self-Government
Act had to be immediately amended. In the event
that the required number of members was not elected
to either the Circle Boards or the District Councils, whose members were elected by the boards,
the Burma government was empowered to nominate members to complete the membership of these bodies.[29]

These apprehensions of inadequate membership
were justified in the case of the Circle Boards
and the effects were felt in the District Councils
where the large number of unfilled seats drew the
attention of the Indian Statutory Commission.[30]

The Circle Boards and District Councils as organs of local self-government failed both as effective instruments for satisfying the needs of the
people and as devices for helping to bring the people of Burma into a working relationship with their
government, which was an essential condition for the

148

developing of effective self-rule in Burma.

The first Municipal Councils in Burma were established in seven municipalities and seven towns
under the Act of 1874 but despite the longer experience they also failed to develop the vitality
of a thriving institution of local self-government.
The presidents of the earlier Municipal Councils
were nominated officials, and it was usually due to
the abilities of this individual that the improvements desired by the Europeans who controlled the
councils were achieved.[31] The majority of the
townspeople either had no need or did not appreciate
the improvements which the European-dominated Municipal Councils sought. Some growing public interest
in the Municipal Council was indicated in the increasing number of nonofficials who served on these
bodies:[32]

	Officials	Nonofficials
1916–1917	200	365
1917–1918	199	363
1918–1919	192	371
1919–1920	192	397

In 1920 the Municipal Councils were made elective
and the number of nonofficials rose to 410 while
the number of officials dropped to 187.[33] The lack
of general public interest was reflected in the de-

pendency of some Municipal Councils upon the European members to keep these bodies functioning. Corruption, which plagued certain Municipal Councils, was also a major impediment to effective town management.

Attendance at Meetings of
Municipal and Town Committees:[34]

	1921-1922	1922-1923	1923-1924
No. of meetings	1043	1281	1371
No. of abortive meetings	15	17	26
Percent of officials present		74.07	41.80
Percent of non-officials present		61.81	60.70

	1924-1925	1925-1926	1926-1927
No. of meetings	1462	1516	1497
No. of abortive meetings	44	32	66
Percent of officials present			
Percent of non-officials present			

	1927-1928
No. of meetings	1444
No. of abortive meetings	72
Percent of officials present	
Percent of non-officials present	

150

The experience with the Municipal Councils in
Burma demonstrated further that institutions of local self-government that are not grounded in the
needs of a politically conscious population cannot
hope to function effectively as a link between the
general public and the government.

Prior to the establishment of British rule,
a measure of popular self-government existed on the
village level in Burma.[35] However, the system of
village administration established after the annexation of Burma caused a decline in these local institutions. The participation of the prepon-
derantly rural Burmese in village affairs was fundamental to the development of the relationship between the people and their government.

The policy of "one village, one headman,"
resulting in the elimination of circle headmen who
were responsible for groups of villages, disrupted
the traditional relationship of the villagers and
their local leaders. The reestablishment of a working relationship between the headman and his people
was essential for the functioning of an effective
village system. Villagers were held jointly responsible for local crime and for failing to defend
the village against criminal attacks by dacoits.
This superimposed joint responsibility was inef-
fective and impeded the growth of genuine civic

responsibility.

In 1917 village government, affecting more than three-fourths of the population, was a mechanistic system manned by headmen who were dissociated from the local population. The idea of common responsibility and mutual self-help had waned.[36] Only in Upper Burma, the last area to come under British rule, were there vestiges of a viable system of village rule.

A comprehensive policy of promoting self-rule in Burma through increasing the association of the populace in the governing process demanded the revitalization of village rule. The area assigned to individual headmen was increased and their income increased.[37] Elected Village Committees were introduced under the Burma Village Amending Act IV (1924) in an effort to close the gap between the people and their government. These Village Committees were designed as general advisory boards to assist headmen. Sitting as judicial bodies, these committees were empowered to try lesser criminal offenses and to hear civil suits involving limited claims.[38] However, these bodies were often out of the stream of the local nationalist movement as were many of the headmen.[39] Because the form of village government was more easily adapted to the needs of a local community, it was the most effective type of local government. Yet the expectations of the political reformers that local self-government would serve as a means of political education and of drawing the people of Burma into the governing process were never realized.

CHAPTER 8

ECONOMIC FOUNDATIONS OF POLITICAL SELF-RULE

The close relationship between the political authority and the economic interests of the ruling
power which characterizes the colonial system was
a further barrier to the development of self-rule
in Burma. The British rulers in Burma maintained
the power to prevent governmental actions on the
part of the Burmese, which the authorities believed
might adversely affect the economic objectives of
British policy. The special responsibilities of
the Governor under the Burma Act of 1935 to maintain
law and order, to safeguard Burma's financial
stability and credit, to protect minorities, and to
prevent economic discrimination reflected the British determination to maintain a check on nationalist forces which might disrupt the prevailing economic pattern.[1] The attempt to maintain the position of British economic interests in Burma impeded
the development of self-rule and barred expansion
of the role of the people of Burma in the economic
life of the country.

The economic grievances of the Burmese, particularly those which grew out of agrarian problems,

at times diverted the nationalist movement into channels that handicapped cooperation between the more moderate Burmese nationalist leaders and British administrators in evolving a viable system of self-rule in Burma. As the nationalist movement gained momentum there was an increasing awareness among Burmese leaders that the transition from the status of a colony to that of a modern state transcended mere political reform. They insisted that Burmese must also take a significant part in the trade and commerce of the country and share more fully in the returns of the national economy. Rice milling, forestry, mining, finance, and trade were all the province of the British, Indians, and other nonindigenous peoples, while approximately 71 percent of the Burmese and other indigenous peoples were engaged in some form of agriculture (1931).[2]

Two associated problems emerged from this dualism in Burma's economy. First was the demand voiced by Burmese nationalists for an increased share in the benefits of the national economy. The Burmese nationalist could contrast the economic lot of the indigenous population with the sizable earnings of British corporations in Burma.[3] The "drain" on Burma's economy represented by the export surplus was Rs. 90,700,000 which almost tripled by 1931-1940 when it reached

Rs. 268,700,000.[4] Despite the rapid economic
advancement of Burma under British rule, the
steady outflow of earnings of British and Indian
capital was a constant reminder to Burmese nationalists that Burma's money economy was largely
in foreign hands.[5]

Significant increments in the share that the
people of Burma received of the national income
depended on greater participation of the indigenous
population in the capital ventures dominated by the
British and Indians. The subsistence type of
economy, which thrived before the advent of
Western enterprises, placed no great value on the
accumulation of liquid capital. Lacking surplus
capital for investment and inexperienced in financial and managerial operations, the people of
Burma witnessed the ultimate controls of the expanding export enterprises of their country devolve
upon the nonindigenous minorities.

There were sound political arguments for nurturing the economic strength of the Burmese and
the development of a middle-class group. An increased stake for the Burmese in the national
economy could strengthen the ranks of political
moderates and might serve as a check on extremism
in the nationalist movement. Furthermore the projected self-ruling Burma could utilize persons

156

experienced in business and finance to carry out
some of the complex economic functions of government. A thoroughgoing policy of political reform
in Burma thus was linked to increased participation
of the Burmese and other peoples of Burma in the
management of the national economy.

A village type economy based on subsistence
agriculture prevailed under the Burmese monarchy.
The farmer was able to provide for his needs from
his lands, supplemented by a few essentials from
the local bazaar. Handicraft industries provided
tools, cloth, pottery, and other necessities for
this local exchange. Foreign trade in rice and
teak was slight prior to the advent of British rule,
while Burma's other resources remained largely
undeveloped. The requirements of the people of
Burma were adequately met by subsistence agriculture supplemented by the products of local
craftsmen.[6]

With the influx of capitalist enterprises,
the focus of Burma's economy shifted from subsistence agriculture to production for export. The
rice export trade, beginning with small shipments
from the coastal provinces that were ceded to the
British after the First Burmese War, rapidly expanded with the development of the productive lower
Irrawaddy basin acquired in 1858. Technological

advances, particularly the opening of the Suez Canal
and the introduction of steam navigation, expanded
the possible markets in Europe for rice and other
commodities from Burma. Burmese migrated from Upper
Burma to settle in the sparsely populated delta region and raise rice to meet the new export demands.
Large rice mills were established in the port cities
to process the paddy (unmilled rice) obtained by
brokers from the cultivators.[7] The Burmese pioneers
in the new rice lands usually had little capital
with which to meet the expenses of clearing the
land, providing water control facilities, and other
initial expenses. Funds were also needed to support
the new cultivator until the returns from the first
harvest were realized. By 1880 the Indian moneylenders began to appear and soon were the chief source
of capital for the agriculturists of the delta region. Annual rice shipments expanded from about
400,000 tons in 1865-1866 to 3,000,000 tons in the
1930s, making Burma the world's leading exporter.[8]

The material conditions of the Burmese peasants
improved substantially with the economic expansion
that accompanied the introduction of Western enterprises. Under the British administration old restrictions on the economic activities of the people
of Burma were removed, and new economic opportunities were made available. Prices for agricultural

158

products rose and new import goods could be pro-
cured.[9] Nevertheless, the rapid expansion of
Burma's economy brought in its wake social disorganization and agrarian problems, which were to
plague efforts at political development.

The Burmese cultivators were able to maintain
a reasonably fair bargaining position in the sale
of rice to the large millers during the 1870s.
With expanding markets, the millers were often
pressed to meet their commitments to the shippers.
By holding back their crops, the cultivators were
at times able to increase the price paid by the
millers. Rice milling for export rapidly became
concentrated in the hands of a few British entrepreneurs, who soon discovered the efficacy of
jointly setting the price they would pay the cultivator for paddy.[10] In 1882 such a joint effort by
the millers kept prices down but at the cost of
severe economic difficulties for many Burmese agriculturists. The Burma government, steeped in
laissez faire traditions, opined that "if the people
were taught by their present experience to erect
mills of their own they would defeat the European
combination and a further step would be taken toward
an equitable adjustment of prices in their favor."[11]
Gradually the European millers in Rangoon expanded
their control over other mills in Burma, which

facilitated collaboration to control the price of paddy paid to the cultivator. The average price paid to the cultivator for rice was gradually forced down from Rs. 127 (1892) to Rs. 77 (1893), despite rising prices for rice on the world market.[12] In the last severe price struggle between the cultivators and the millers in 1894, the millers came off holding the upper hand, which they were able to maintain thereafter.[13] This pattern of development, repeated with variations in other aspects of Burma's economy, led to the domination of export industries by nonindigenous minorities and provoked the nationalist demands for a greater share in the benefits of the country's economy.

Though the European millers in Rangoon virtually controlled the processing of rice for export, a number of small mills were established in the interior to serve local needs. These small mills were owned by the Indians, Chinese, and Burmese. While the number of mills in the port cities of Rangoon, Akyab, and Moulmein increased from 72 to 94 in the period 1900-1930, the number of small rice mills in the interior jumped from 27 to 528. However, these mills serving local needs could handle only an average of from 10 to 75 tons daily, while the large mills at the marine shipping centers could handle from 200 to 500 hundred tons daily.

160

By 1939 most of the mills were owned by Burmese and other indigenous peoples, who operated small plants in the interior. Nevertheless the great bulk of rice continued to pass through the port millers, chiefly Europeans.[14] Though the Burmese were beginning to participate in the rice industry in other capacities than that of cultivators, they still had made no inroads into the export trade and, by and large, were confined to local businesses.

The important teak industry was dominated by four large European companies that held long-term leases from the government giving them the right to extract this important export commodity. The policy of the administration was to earmark the more accessible areas for small traders, while the more inaccessible areas requiring more capital for exploitation were assigned to European firms.[15] Besides an Indo-Burmese firm holding a long-term lease there were a number of very small locally owned enterprises. A similar pattern of ownership prevailed in sawmilling. About 75 percent of the teak output was extracted by five European firms.[16]

The oil fields of Burma had been worked by the Burmese prior to the establishment of British firms to extract petroleum by modern techniques. These Burmese operators enjoyed hereditary rights in the oil fields and produced for the limited local needs.

The Burmah Oil Company first bought crude oil from the Burmese drillers but by 1887 were extracting petroleum directly. The large capital demands of petroleum extraction and processing soon eliminated all but a few corporations, the most important of which, the Burmah Oil Company, was responsible for 75 percent of the colony's production immediately prior to World War II.[18] The Burmese, utilizing primitive techniques, quickly lost out of modern technology. Efforts by the nationalists of the Home Rule Party to induce the public of Burma to take shares in modern oil refining ventures met with little success.[19] Some local people were trained as drillers, but the indigenous population took no significant part in the management or ownership of the petroleum industry. The mining of silver, lead, zinc, tin, and tungsten was also practically all controlled by British corporations.

A pressing demand of the nationalists was for industralization, which they equated with improved economic conditions for the Burmese. The few large factories in Burma were owned by Europeans, Indians, and Chinese, as were a considerable number of the smaller workshops. Faced with the competition of cheaper imported goods, the handicraft industries of Burma had declined greatly in importance. . The government attempted to resuscitate three of these

162

so-called cottage industries: weaving, pottery, and lacquer working.

A Legislative Council resolution proposing government assistance to new industries in Burma resulted in a loan to the Burma Spinning and Weaving Company. This business which had been initiated by two residents of India, was managed by a board of directors made up of persons from Burma who were also the principal stockholders. A smaller number of shares were held by about two thousand persons in all parts of Burma. Though the company was in poor financial condition, it was granted a loan of Rs. 1,500,000 on the motion of the opposition in the Legislative Council.[20] The company was unable to meet interest payments on the government loan and in November, 1926, requested that the government attach all its property in satisfaction of the debt. This was done and eventually the plant was taken over by one of the major British corporaations.[21] The loan to the Burma Spinning and Weaving Company was the principal effort by the Burma government to establish Burmese in industry on any large scale. Of the 1,007 factories registered in pre-World War II Burma, one-seventh of them employing one-half of the industrial workers in Burma were owned by Europeans.[22] Not only had the Burmese failed to participate in the ownership of a limited

163

number of industries but local handicrafts had lost ground to imported manufactures.

Trade and banking were similarly under the control of the Europeans, Indians, and Chinese. About three-quarters of the 5,500,000 pounds invested in trade and banking in Burma were British holdings.[23] The small moneylenders, chiefly Indians of the Chettyar caste, extended loans to the peasant cultivators at annual interest rates of from 15 to 45 percent.[24] The Burmese peasant, once enmeshed in heavy debts, was frequently unable to extricate himself, and control of much of the land in Lower Burma passed out of the hands of the cultivator.

Land Occupancy in Lower Burma[25]

	Total Area Occupied	Area Held by Non-agriculturists	Area Held by Chettyars
1930	9,249,000	2,943,000	570,000
1937	9,650,000	4,929,000	2,446,000

The Burmese had usually prevailed in the local trade in foodstuffs, handicraft articles, and other necessities, while the Indians and Chinese monopolized the trade in the imported commodities, which were finding an increasing market in Burma. Although the Burmese began to take a greater role in the merchandizing of such commodities in the decade prior to World War II, the Indians and Chinese had the advantage of experience and established

164

connections in these businesses.

Even the limited number of establishments owned
and managed by Burmese were small enterprises. In
1927 about 73 percent of the industries owned by
indigenous peoples were rice mills and another 16
percent sawmills.

Race of Owners of Establishments (1927)[26]

	Number of Establishments	
Race	Private Owner	Companies
Indigenous and Indo-Burman races	287	22
Indians	106	22
Others	104	186
Total	497	230

Race of Managers

	All Industries	Important Industries
Indigenous and Indo-Burman races	44	44
Europeans and Anglo-Indians	20	24
Indians	36	17
Others		15

Economic nationalism usually was directed
the Indians who had personal dealings with the Burmese rather than against the more remote British
enterprises. Indian moneylenders were to be found
in many of the villages of Burma while the British

165

holdings were concentrated in Rangoon or at the oil fields, mines, and sawmills where comparatively few Burmese were aware of their operations. The most real manifestation of British power to the Burmese peasant was the government official who collected taxes, enforced regulations, and provided welfare services for the villages. The more politically conscious nationalist leaders were cognizant of the overall colonial pattern of Burma's economy in which nonindigenous population formed the economic elite. Aside from measures directed against the Indians, the economic issues seized upon by the Burmese nationalists were generalized in demands for the economic development of the country, the improvement of education, and training for the indigenous peoples and the reduction of foreign exploitation.[28]

The Burmese nationalists had taken the initiative in obtaining government financial assistance for the Burma Spinning and Weaving Company. Prior to 1929 only four questions were put to the government in the Legislative Council on other measures taken for industrial development in Burma. These inquiries suggested government aid in launching salt, pottery, and sugar industries. These few suggestions were repeated in debates on the budget.[29] On the whole, the early Burmese nationalists were primarily interested in political reform.

166

The economic hardships of the early 1930s highlighted by the rebellion of 1931-1932, brought
greater emphasis on demands for an increased share
in the control and benefits of the major industries
which produced for export. At the Burma Round Table
Conference, the Burmese nationalists emphasized the
necessity of political reform as a means to economic
reform. U Su of the GCBA, speaking "on behalf of
the masses of Burma," condemned the Burma government
as being "entirely for the welfare and interests of
a small number of capitalists." No solution to
the "peasant revolution" of 1931-1932 could be attained without "overthrowing foreign exploitation."
Since British rule was alien to the interests of
the people of Burma, U Su concluded, it was necessary to place "full and complete responsibility in
the hands of the masses of Burma."[30] This increasing attention to the economic consequences of
British rule broadened the attack of the Burmese
nationalists in their campaign for self-rule.

The nationalists of the 1930s, speaking from
wider experience and broader exposure to Western
ideas than most of their predecessors, spelled out
more specific demands for economic reforms. U Ba Pe
and other moderates proposed before the Joint Committee on Indian Constitutional Reform that local
enterprise be encouraged by requiring that corpora-

167

tions holding contracts from the government meet
minimum requirements for Burmese participation. U
Ba Pe's plan called for a contract-holding corporation to insure that persons from Burma have an un-
specified percentage of the shares of its stock,
places on its board of directors, positions as workers for the corporation, and also that such persons
receive training for responsible positions in the
business.[31]

From the inception of British rule in Burma,
the British administration directed its efforts to
the economic development of the colony. Even during
the period of laissez faire, the emphasis in British
policy rested on assuring an environment conducive
to economic expansion. As Lieutenant-Governor Sir
Harcourt Butler appraised the situation in 1916,
"Burma can only be developed with the aid of, /and/
largely by means of, private enterprise, and that
private enterprise needs security, encouragement and
a prospect of profit commensurate with the risks
involved."[32] However realistic this attitude was,
it failed to relate the program of economic development of Burma to the economic and political development of the people of Burma.

Limited efforts were made by the Burma government to stimulate indigenous enterprise. Upon the
recommendation of the Indian Industrial Commission,

a Department of Industries was organized in 1921.
A Development Commissioner was placed in charge of
this new department which was to direct its major
efforts to promoting small-scale cottage industries.
The lack of experience, training, and capital were
the principal deterrents to the establishment of
industries by the Burmese. The Industrial Finance
Committee, established by the Burma government,
undertook the task of finding means whereby new
industries might be started with government assistance. Industries connected with agriculture, such
as rice milling, should be given a priority claim
on financial aid, the committee recommended, although other industries might be supported if
"reasonable" programs for their development were
set forth. The Industrial Finance Committee recommended three forms of government aid for new industries. The Burma government circumvented the
recommendation that "infant industries" be exempted
from rents and royalties and that they be granted
leases on land on favorable terms. The suggestion
that the new enterprises be exempted from taxes on
profits and that import duty on articles utilized
in such industries be remitted was dismissed as
outside the authority of the provincial government.
The proposal by the Industrial Finance Committee
that the government extend loans to the fledgling

enterprises was accepted by the British administrators. The Burma government indicated its willingness to assist the sugar, pottery, and cotton spinning trades. This led directly to the ill-starred venture of the Burma Spinning and Weaving Corporation.[33] To follow through with its recommendations, the Industrial Finance Committee called for the formation of a permanent Advisory Board of Industries but this proposal was set aside by the government in favor of ad hoc committees for specific problems of development. The government attempted to increase the role of the Burmese in the non-agricultural economic activities of the country by promoting cottage industries. The serious handicaps under which such cottage industries as weaving operated were recognized. The extension of handicraft types of activities depended largely on improved marketing methods combined with standardization of output.

Cooperative societies, designed primarily to provide credit to agriculturalists, were also used to promote small industries among the indigenous population. A group of individuals wishing to start a cooperative enterprise could register their cooperative with the Burma government and become eligible to borrow funds from special banks backed by the government. No government funds were used

to initiate these ventures but advisors were provided by the local administration, which also
inspected the societies. The cooperative societies
involved in making loans to agriculturists were
generally more successful than those organized as
business ventures. Rice mills were established
under the cooperative program, but they were usually
small and lacked sufficient financial reserves to
tide them over difficult periods. In the fiscal
year 1922-1923 the cooperative Wethlagale Rice Mill
lost Rs. 14,604, and further losses the next year
wiped the mill out. The Salt Boiler societies
were dissolved when it became apparent that they
were unable to meet foreign competition. Weaving
societies faced difficult problems in marketing.
Small cotton ginneries launched as cooperatives
soon foundered. Even the more long-lived business
cooperatives never acquired large proportions. The
Legaing Rice Milling Society was only producing
132,400 baskets of rice annually after five years of
operation (1923-1928) which was infinitesimal compared to the output of the large British—owned mills
in Rangoon. The depression of the 1930s delivered
the coup d'grace to many of these faltering cooperative societies and crippled the government program
which had been designed to promote small indigenous
industries in Burma. The failure of the coopera-

tive system to develop local industries was owing to shortcomings on all sides. The government was cautious about even indirect financial backing for the societies and the cooperatives often limped along with inadequate capital at their disposal.[34] The advisors appointed by the government to assist the cooperatives were themselves often inexperienced or unable to give adequate attention to the societies' problems.[35] The managers of the cooperatives were generally inexperienced and unable to cope with the problems of operating a new industry with inadequate capital in the face of established competition. One after another the cooperative societies organized for production and sales fell apart. Conceived on a limited scale, the government's policy for the promotion of indigenous industries through cooperative societies proved inadequate to the task.[36]

The Burmese were unable to penetrate the large-scale export industries owned and operated by the minority groups and even the handicraft industries lost out to imported manufactures. Lacking adequate capital and business experience, the Burmese were unable to share in the direction of their national economy.[37]

The prolonged wrangle over the disbursement of rice control profits strikingly illustrated the di-

172

vergent concepts of Burma's economic interests that existed between the British administration and the people of Burma and also between the India and Burma governments. In 1918 and 1919, the government of India, operating through a Rice Control Board, established a temporary monopoly on the export of rice. The objective was primarily to prevent the domestic price of rice from following the soaring world market price of rice. The differential between the price paid by the government to millers and brokers and the price received from the sale abroad was placed in a special fund. The India government attempted to divert all but Rs. 10,000,000 of this fund, amounting to Rs. 91,752,000, for the reduction of India's floating debt or otherwise for the benefit of India as a whole.[38] The Burma government contested the central administration on the issue and was supported by the Meston Committee, which was investigating the financial relations between the provincial and central governments. The committee, pointing out that Burma was "far behind India proper in what its Government does for the people," recommended that the rice-control profits should be devoted to promote internal developments within the province.[39]

The government of India conceded in April, 1920, and approved the allocation of all profits

from the rice control program to the Burma government, providing that the funds could be profitably
expended for the benefit of the cultivators. Within
this general limitation the provincial government
was given considerable latitude. The funds did not
have to be spent in those districts where rice was
raised for export. A scramble for the division of
the rice control profits ensued within the Burma
government. All development programs involving such
recurring costs, as those in education and sanitation, were eliminated.[40] An advisory committee
on the allocation of Rice-Control Profits, consisting of eleven Europeans and seven persons from
Burma, accepted the tentative conclusion advanced
by the administration that one-quarter of the funds
be used for railroad development. While this type
of expenditure was explained as a means of "increasing the realizable price," which the peasant
might receive for his rice, it was more directly
related to the interests of the large corporations
since paddy was usually transported via waterways,
a cheaper means of transportation than the railroads.
About one-half of the funds was to be used for the
more immediate needs of the agricultural population.

174

Allocation of Rice-Control Profits[41]

	Rs.
Railroads	22,500,000
Roads	27,500,000
Embankment of flood protection	7,500,000
Agricultural and veterinary improvements	7,500,000
Improvement of navigable waterways	2,500,000
Improvement of water supplies	2,500,000
Measures for improvement of the economic conditions of agriculturists	10,000,000
Irrigation works	10,000,000
Total	90,000,000

The improvement of agrarian conditions was primarily directed toward the improvement of rural credit facilities. The extension of railways and the improvement of roads, while fostering the overall economic development of Burma, were more immediately related to the transport requirements of the large export industries than to the pressing needs of the Burmese peasant for agrarian rehabilitation.

The Burmese nationalists became increasingly insistent on greater participation in the returns from and management of their country's economy. The British administration was committed to a policy of turning over political powers to the people of Burma, while at the same time it was expected to

175

support the maintenance of the British economic position in Burma. This dilemma persisted and hobbled the development of self-rule in Burma by restricting the assumption of political responsibility by the people of Burma and by impairing the wider participation of indigenous peoples in the national economy.

CHAPTER 9

BRITISH POLICY IN THE BALANCE

Burma remained a political backwater prior to the
reform movement of 1917, removed from the main currents of nationalism which were gaining momentum
in India. On the surface there were few indications
of the internal dissatisfactions that would seek
redress through political action. The peoples of
Burma enjoyed better living conditions on the whole
than did the other peoples of India. [Buddhism,
the most pervasive social force in Burma, eschewed
violence and encouraged the contemplative approach
to human problems.] The Burmese were traditionally
regarded as a rather carefree, easygoing people with
little interest in events beyond their villages.
Yet by 1917 there were already the undercurrents of
agrarian discontent and social unrest which, with
the growing currents of modern nationalism, would
eventually undercut British control in Burma.

These economic and social problems were the
heritage of the precipitate union of the Western
political and economic institutions with the traditional Burmese society consummated during the
nineteenth century under the aegis of British rule.

British policy in Burma did not provide means for cushioning the impact of Western institutions on Burmese society. Rather the policies carried out by the British administration heightened the impact of modern economic and political institutions on the people of Burma.

The colonial relationship which Burma bore to Great Britain established the general framework within which British policy operated. The primary task of the British administration in Burma was to insure conditions conducive to economic expansion along lines consistent with British interests. Initially, under the influence of laissez faire and nineteenth-century liberalism, such a policy meant the removal of restrictions on economic activity, the expansion of individual freedoms, the intro-duction of a money economy, and the institution of a Western type of legal system. The government di-rected itself to maintaining internal order, admin-istrative efficienty and financial stability. The village system was regularized to establish lines of responsibility for the collection of revenues and the maintenance of law and order. Gradually the government assumed a more direct role in the economic development of Burma. Beginnings were made in the innovation of public works and welfare programs. Nominal checks were placed on the exploitation of natural resources. Measures were introduced to protect the position of the peasant cultivator. The overriding policy considerations were, however, in almost all cases, the encouragement of economic development and the promotion of administrative efficiency.

The manifest results of less than a century of British rule in Burma were impressive. The population of the country had expanded rapidly. Economic activities had increased in magnitude and variety. The development of the rice areas of the lower Irrawaddy basin was a particularly impressive example of the potentialities of the Burmese peasant under stable British administration. Burma's trade, particularly her exports, accelerated rapidly. The revenues of the government increased to comfortable levels. The people of Burma were freed from many of the traditional restrictions of the Burmese regime and were able to secure new imported manufactures that appeared in the local markets. The material returns appeared to justify the British policies in Burma.

The long-run results of these policies did not become fully apparent until the 1917-1937 period, when mounting crime, absentee landlordism, agricultural tenancy, rural indebtedness, hostility to foreign economic interests, and social instability

179

testified to the detrimental effects of policies in
which economic expansion and administrative efficiency are the primary objectives. The agrarian discontent and social instability, which proceeded
from the early British policies in Burma, impeded
the whole process of developing self-rule during the
1917-1937 period of political reform.

The modern nationalist movement in Burma,
though precipitated by the innovations of political
reform in India in 1917, stemmed in large measure
from the special conditions which prevailed in Burma. The cultural homogeneity and still extant
political traditions of the Burmese provided the
crucible within which the various components of the
nationalist movement were eventually solidified
into an effective force. Western institutions and
ideologies were particularly significant components
contributing to the shaping of the nationalist
movement in Burma. The Burmese encountered these
new concepts either directly through their experience with the British institutions in Burma or
indirectly through contact with the other nationalist movements in Asia. Current ideas about national self-determination and a growing awareness of
the potentialities of social change gave impetus
to nascent nationalism in Burma. Increasing dissatisfaction with economic conditions offered a

180

wide field for nationalist leadership to gain popular support for their programs of political reform.
For this purpose the Burmese nationalist leaders
could utilize the forms and instrumentalities of
political action offered by the newly encountered
Western institutions and ideologies. ⌈In this manner
the political innovations introduced by the British
rulers in Burma were turned against them in the
nationalist struggle for self-rule and eventual
independence.⌋

The modern nationalist movement in Burma
initially encompassed only a few politically conscious Burmese who had been exposed to the new concepts of national self-determination. The dissatisfactions of the villagers found expression in measures designed to frustrate British administrative
controls and to dislodge foreign economic interests.
The nationalist leaders were able to harness popular
opposition to the government to the movement for
self-rule only after the new ideologies had been
linked to the expectations, desires, and sense of
national identity of the Burmese villagers.

Theravada Buddhism was the religion of most
of the inhabitants of Burma. The early expressions
of Burmese nationalism were directed to issues involving the prestige and sanctity of the Buddhist
faith. The Buddhist _pongyis_ were the agents for

the spread of nationalism on the village level. Generally, the British administrators exercised great discretion in dealing with Buddhism. The few conspicuous cases in which repressive measures were used against <u>pongyis</u> provoked strong popular dis-affection for the British regime.

The Burmese nationalists were at first pre-occupied with institutional political reform. The degree of self-rule which they sought gradually expanded. Prior to the 1923 reforms the main concern of the nationalists was to see that Burma received as extensive self-rule as was granted to India. During the interreform period, home rule or local autonomy became the rallying call of the more demanding nationalists. By the 1930s, when further reforms were under consideration, the Burmese nationalists had raised the stakes to dominion status. The accelerating pace of nationalist political demands placed severe strains on the British policy of gradualism in introducing political reforms.

The amorphous political groupings that were the vanguard of Burmese nationalism centered around a few key individuals who adapted their political programs to the situations in which they operated. There were numerous splits and regroupings of political parties that militated against the existence
182

of stable political groups willing and able to cooperate with the British in working for limited,
gradual reforms. Two basic disagreements among the
Burmese nationalists prevented the consolidation
of the nationalist movement. The noncooperators
refused to participate in the dyarchical system of
government established in 1923 to promote the gradual development of self-rule. Other nationalists
chose to seek their political objectives within the
framework established by the British policy makers.
The second major difference among the nationalists
was on the question of separation from India. In
general the same group of more extreme nationalist
leaders who had opposed participation in the government attempted to block the immediate separation of
Burma from India, anticipating that Burma would be
denied the reforms extended to the people of India.
The schismatic character of the political groupings
in Burma and the disagreements on these two major
issues essentially represented differences in methods of approaching a common goal--accession to
political power. While the differences and rival-
ries within the nationalist camp strengthened the
hand of the British administration by dissipating
the strength of the nationalist movement, these
conditions also prevented the development of well-
established responsible groups with whom the ad-

ministration could deal.

The tactics and practices of the nationalists of almost all persuasions also impeded British policy for the development of self-rule. Some of these tactics, such as the boycott of elections, were undertaken in the name of advancing nationalist objectives. Other practices, such as the use of public office for self-benefit, tended to discredit the limited institutions for self-government the British were trying to encourage. As a whole, the performance of the Burmese politicians and those from other indigenous groups did not inspire great confidence among the politically conscious public, or among the British either, as to their ability to provide effective leadership in a self-governing Burma.

The British policy makers and administrators gave their principal attention to the development of political institutions that would permit the people of Burma to take a gradually expanding role in the government, while permitting the British administrators to maintain sufficient powers in reserve to cope with any situation detrimental to British interests. At the same time, the new political institutions had to lend themselves to effective government for everyday operations and to give promise of providing a viable system of self-rule

184

when the leaders of Burma assumed full responsibility for the government of their country. In several of their aspects, these differing purposes for which political institutions were devised were not consistent, and consequently the institutions did not meet all the tests to which they were exposed.

The Montagu declaration of 1917 sounded the keynote for the British policy of political reform. Self-governing institutions would be developed with a view to the progressive realization of responsible government within the empire. While the methods and timing by which the British sought to implement this policy occasionally shifted, these objectives remained valid throughout the period of political reform.

Burma's position as a province of the Indian empire protracted the process of decision making for constitutional reform and often stymied policy implementation. The policy-making process for Burma involved three levels of government from Rangoon through New Delhi to London. Too often the special conditions which prevailed in Burma were ignored in forming overall policy for India. The question of separation from India provoked further acrimony in an already complex political situation.

The dyarchical system of government was devised as a means of gradually bringing about responsible government through a flexible approach to the distribution of executive authority. Dyarchy was acknowledged to be a failure as a mechanism of political training. The ministers from Burma exercising the authority transferred to them from the executive were dependent to a considerable extent on the senior civil servants of their departments which retarded the development of real authority and self-reliance on the part of the ministers. The ministers and the Governor's Executive Councillors administering the reserved subjects did not form a cohesive cabinet-type of government. There were no effective means whereby the members of the Legislative Council could hold the ministers responsible for their actions. From its inception, dyarchy was hampered by the noncooperation movement. From an administrative point of view, dyarchy proved to be a workable, but at times awkward, system of government.

The constitutional structure devised for Burma in 1935 was less contrived than the dyarchical system and provided a suitable framework for developing greater ministerial responsibility in Burma. The Governor retained a wide range of powers, but within the limits of their responsibility, the ministers from Burma could evolve effective policies directed

toward meeting the needs of the people of Burma.
The Governor remained the control mechanism for
safeguarding the interests of the British rulers
and for expanding the role of the Burmese and other
indigenous peoples in the government.

The political institutions devised for Burma
failed to provide the Burmese and their countrymen
with experience in important functions of government. Foreign relations and defense remained central subjects under the 1923 reforms. Under the
1935 constitution, these subjects were reserved for
the Governor. However, Burma did receive advances
denied to the other provinces of India, in 1923,
when the administration of forests and education
were transferred to local ministers. British policy
gave officials from Burma numerous opportunities
to gain administrative experience in the "nation-
building" branches of the government.

The evolution of institutions of self-government in Burma was impeded by special conditions in
the political process in Burma. The nonindigenous
minorities, whose economic importance far surpassed
their numerical strength, clamored for special
political representation. Status quo elements within the British community opposed many of the measures for bringing the Burmese into the government.
Obstructionism from Burmese nationalists hampered

187

the operation of political institutions. The Burma
government was subject to control from New Delhi
and consequently was limited in its policies. In
the face of these difficulties the political institutions evolved in Burma provided the elements
for a viable system of government, though they
proved inadequate as instruments for political development in the sense of preparing people for self-
government.

The increasing association of the indigenous
population in the administration of the government
as a method of promoting self-rule was a basic
principle of the British policy statement of 1917.
The necessity for recruiting a bureaucracy from
among the people of Burma, if effective self-rule
was to be instituted, was particularly apparent.
Prior to 1917, indigenous people held no important
posts in the administration, though many of the
minor positions in rural areas were filled by Burmese and other local peoples. The preparation of
the people of Burma to hold responsible civil service positions in the government was a necessary
complement to policies designed to provide indigenous political leadership.

The process of Burmanization of the civil
services, as it was called, faced several serious
handicaps. For one thing, the British could not

188

meet the problems by disproportionate recruitment among indigenous people per se, even though some of the minority groups might have been more cooperative and amendable to British policy. It was necessary to concentrate on the majority group, the Burmese. There were an insufficient number of Burmese with the type of education that would enable them to compete successfully with university-trained British and Indian candidates on the civil service examinations. Most of the Burmese who were successful in the civil service rose to positions of moderate importance only after long service in lower posts. The better educated British and Indians held most of the higher positions. Corruption among Burmese and other indigenous officials discouraged the process of Burmanization. The entrenched members of the Indian Civil Service resisted encroachments on their positions from the indigenous population.

While the number of officials from Burma in the lower ranks of the civil service roughly doubled during this period of political development, there was not a proportionate increase in the higher ranks. An effective policy of Burmanization required more intensive programs in education and apprenticeship than were carried out. Burma faced a period of greater self-rule with an inadequate number of its citizens trained for government service.

The pluralistic colonial society, which prevailed in Burma, characterized by the concentration
of economic and political power in the hands of nonindigenous minorities, was a major obstacle to the
development of a viable nation-state. A comprehensive policy for the development of responsible
self-government would eschew actions which might
deepen this cleavage in society in Burma and seek
out programs to eliminate this barrier to national
unity.

The differences among the indigenous ethnic
groups in Burma seemed at that time to present no
major obstacles to the development of a unified
Burma. The Karens were one possible source of dis-
sension. Karen loyalty to the British heightened
earlier antagonisms that existed with the Burmese.
Though they enjoyed separate representation in the
legislature, the basic interests of the Karens and
the Burmese seemed to be reconcilable.

The nonindigenous minorities comprising the
political and economic elite in the pluralistic
society were the most apparent deterrents to the
evolution of an economically integrated Burma.
The Indian population in Burma presented special
problems. Indian commercial interests and moneylenders held a firm grip on much of Burma's economy,

190

particularly with reference to the rice lands of the lower Irrawaddy basin. Indian labor offered effective competition to the increasing number of Burmese wage laborers. These economic problems found expression in growing Burmese antagonism toward the Indians and mounting social and political tensions.

The policies pursued by the British administration in Burma with regard to minorities, both indigenous and nonindigenous, tended to perpetuate the existing pluralistic pattern of society in Burma. Economic and administrative considerations were often decisive in determining the attitude of the Burma government toward minority groups. The interests of minority groups were forwarded by the policies of the government at times at the expense of the Burmese. The political strength of the British and Indian minorities in Burma reflected their economic position rather than their numbers. The more important minorities and economic interests were given special representation in the legislature. This system of communal representation institutionalized group differences and militated against the development of a unified population in Burma.

The Governor was given special responsibilities to safeguard the minorities in Burma, and special constitutional measures were devised to insure the

minorities against discrimination. In handling
minority problems, the Burma government tried to
balance the influence of the minorities in Burma
against the nationalism of the Burmese majority.
This policy tended to accentuate differences between the Burmese and the minorities and militated
against the development of a comprehensive sense of
national unity.

Separation from India was a basic requisite for
responsible self-government in Burma. As a province
Burma had no foreign relations, and defense policy
was determined by the central government in India.
The Burma government, the greater part of the
British community in Burma, and the Burmese nationalists advocated separation although nationalist
elements tied separation to minimum political reforms. By severing Burma's ties to Indian tariff
and immigration policies, taxation and government
spending could be more directly aligned with the
interests of Burma rather than with the broader considerations of Indian policy. British policy makers
were fully aware of Burma's anomalous position as an
Indian province and, despite some reluctance on the
part of the Indian government, anticipated the
separation of Burma, which was effected in The
Government of Burma Act of 1935.

By recruiting minority groups almost to the

exclusion of the Burmese, the British administration failed to develop a military force in Burma in which the major indigenous group played a significant role. The British policy for military recruitment in Burma delayed the development of an effective Burmese military force under Burmese leadership, an essential element for a self-governing Burma.

The effective operation of the institutions for responsible self-government devised for Burma required increased public interest and participation in the political process. The apathy of the people of Burma toward institutional political reform was only slowly overcome during the 1917-1937 period and remained a deterrent to the functioning of government on all levels.

The people of Burma were given a relatively broad suffrage under the 1923 reforms, though they had had no preparation in the use of the ballot. This liberal franchise was not effectively employed, and the Burmese and their countrymen either remained politically indifferent or consciously shunned the polls under the boycott instituted by nationalist leaders prior to 1932. Abuses of the franchise by dishonest politicians and voters further detracted from the value of the ballot as a method of political education in Burma. The generous franchise accorded to the people of Burma by the British policy makers, dictated in part by reasons of administrative expediency, did not generate the type of response that would signal broad popular participation in the political process--a necessary step in the development of self-government.

Under the British rule the people of Burma were afforded a wide range of personal liberties consistent with Western liberal tradition, but these liberties were not always meaningful to the people concerned. The Burma government retained the power to infringe upon personal liberties in the interests of law and order, and serious restrictions were placed on the rights of the individual in times of emergency. The conditional nature of some of the personal liberties, particularly with regard to the judicial process, impaired the development of confidence in the government by the politically conscious among the Burmese and other indigenous peoples.

The British administration placed considerable emphasis on the processes of local self-government as instruments for increasing public participation in government and for affording opportunities for gaining political experience and training. The Circle Boards and District Councils failed both as effective organs of government and as institutions for political training due to public indifference,

194

nationalist hostility, and excessive supervision from the provincial government. The Municipal Councils were directed to the needs of the European population, which took an active interest in the operation of these bodies. The Burmese gradually assumed a wider role in the government of towns and cities, but the Municipal Councils were not significant in bringing the people of Burma into the process of local self-government.

The system of village administration, introduced by the British during the nineteenth century, displaced the traditional authority of the local officials with a mechanistic type of organization devised to meet the needs of the provincial government. The consequent social disorganization multiplied the difficulties of developing self-rule in Burma. Attempts made to rectify conditions of village government through the introduction of village committees in 1924 were generally unsuccessful. Nevertheless, because the Burmese and other indigenous peoples were more immediately interested in the affairs of the village and because forms were often adapted to meet the needs of local conditions, the system of village government proved to be the most effective means of increasing popular participation in local government.

The Burmese nationalists were increasingly

concerned with the problems presented by the colonial pattern of Burma's economy. The ownership and management of the major export industries were concentrated in the hands of the nonindigenous minorities. The Burmese were principally farmers with only very limited interests in trade in local commodities. The lack of adequate capital and managerial experience retarded the development of Burmese enterprises on a large scale and consequently there was no indigenous middle-class that might have influenced the development of responsible self-government in Burma. The principal effort by the government to encourage major indigenously owned and operated industries was poorly conceived and soon failed. Attention was given more successfully to the development of small cottage industries. The few rice mills and cotton ginneries organized under the government's cooperative association program lacked both adequate capital and capable management and proved unsuccessful. The British administration was dedicated to the economic development of Burma, which could most effectively be carried out by large-scale corporations with ample foreign capital. The Burmese remained excluded from the major export industries, which dominated Burma's economy.

The British policy for developing self-rule in Burma was introduced under portentous circumstances.

196

The growing social and economic problems in rural areas which, in part resulted from the impact of Western institutions, denied the newly conceived organs of self-government of the requisite internal stability for their effective operation. The indifference of the majority of Burmese to the Western type of political reforms and the skepticism of the British community in Burma impaired the formation of constructive public opinion.

The tenuous chain of responsibility running from the village through the district to Rangoon, thence to New Delhi, and finally to London made for discrepancies in policy and for political setbacks due to delays in reform.

The British administration in Burma made notable contributions to the political advancement of Burma by Western criteria: the high standards of the civil service, the emphasis on personal freedoms, the institutions of parliamentary government among many others. Yet these features of British rule in Burma were not adequately adapted to the peculiar needs of the situation in Burma and were too often conceived of with an eye solely to effective administration.

British policy for the development of self-rule in Burma was but one of the policies determining the operation of the British administration in Burma. Consequently the political advancement of the Burmese often suffered in the interest of other considerations in overall British policy. Furthermore, the policy for the development of self-rule was restricted in scope and did not systematically treat all relevant problems that were raised by the prospect of responsible self-government in Burma. Considering the limitations within which British policy was conceived and allowing for the unfavorable political climate in which it operated, the British administration had evolved a viable constitutional apparatus with which the people of Burma could undertake the government of their country. Yet effective self-government transcends institutional forms, and it was here that British policy demonstrated its greatest shortcomings. The Burmese and other peoples of Burma faced political independence equipped with the institutional forms for self-rule but were inadequately prepared to meet the manifold problems which self-government thrust upon them.

APPENDICES

APPENDIX A

THE FUNCTIONING OF

THE BRITISH ADMINISTRATION IN BURMA

A DESCRIPTION BY A BRITISH OFFICIAL

"In most towns of Burma there was a jail, a police
station, a hospital and a school. An English official lived there, a person called the Deputy Commissioner. His duty was to cause the police to
arrest those who broke the law and to bring them
before him, when he passed judgment upon them according to the evidence. From time to time he inspected the hospital and the school. His other
main duty was to collect the revenue, which he
partly used to pay his salary and to pay for the
jail, the police, the hospital and the school. The
inhabitants grew rice, some of which they ate,
selling the remainder and buying with the proceeds
clothes, other foods, medicines and household
necessities, and paying the revenue."

Source: Maurice Collis, "The Burma Scene," Geo-
         graphical Magazine, Volume 7 (1938),
         p. 409.

APPENDIX B

ORDER FOR THE CONFISCATION OF SEDITIOUS LITERATURE
ISSUED BY THE GOVERNMENT OF BURMA
AUGUST 29, 1927

The Governor in Council ordered forfeited a "Burmese
Leaflet dated 8th Waning of Wagaung, 1289 B.E.,
calling upon all Burman Buddhists and all monks who
owe allegiance to the All-Burma Sangha Council, to
convene mass meetings at all towns and villages with
a view to performing religious rites on behalf of
the deceased U Sandima and to recite aloud three
times the words, 'Do you think we will forget the
lawlessness of the English people until the end of
the world,' and to meditate upon the law of im-
permance the rest of the day as a sign of sorrow
for the loss of Pongyi U Sandima in Mandalay printed
at Kawperja Press, West Lammadaw, Gyobingauk, and
published by U Wimalasarn, In-charge-of-office, Wunthanu District Council, Tharrawaddy" for containing
seditious literature punishable under section 124A
Indian Penal Code as tending to excite disaffection
towards Government.

Source: Burma Gazette, Part I, 1927, p. 921.

APPENDIX C

MEMORANDUM BY THE BURMA (BRITISH) CHAMBER

OF COMMERCE ON POLITICAL REFORM--1929

Basic conditions for political reform:

1. The form of government must be as simple
as possible.

2. The official element must be retained in
responsible executive positions.

3. Police administration must not be made a
transferred subject.

4. British elements in the civil services
must not be reduced below the minimums laid down
by the Lee Commission.

5. Seats must be reserved for the minorities
and special interests in the legislature.

"Finally this Chamber desires to repeat that
in making these recommendations it is influenced
solely by its desire for peace, prosperity and good
government in Burma. It does not ask for British
Commerce any special privileges, at the same time
it claims protection for the legitimate interests
which its members have built up and developed by
their enterprise and capital. It hopes to see the
country so developed that the greatest benefit may

be derived by all from its natural resources, and the political aspirations of the people fulfilled to the utmost degree compatible with the safety of commercial interests."

Source: Great Britain, Indian Statutory Commission, Volume XVII, Selections from Memoranda and Oral Evidence by Non-Officials, p. 361.

APPENDIX D

BU ATHIN OATH

"From to-day to the end of my life and so long as
Home Rule is not attained, I will work for Home
Rule heart and soul without flinching from duties
even if my bones are crushed and my skin torn; if I
fail to work for Home Rule, may I die on land from
the dangers of land, and on water from the dangers
of water, may I suffer in Hell permanently just
as permanently as the stump of a tree sticking out
of the ground. I will not bid for fisheries or
(government licensed) shops; I will not drink intoxicating liquor or take to opium; I will not cooperate with the Government; if I co-operate with
the Government may I suffer in Hell permanently;
if a member of a Bu Athin is in trouble and requires
my assistance I will help him, not avoiding the sun
or rain, without wearing umbrella or shoes; I will
not use the wearing apparel of foreign make, I will
not marry foreigners; if a member of a Bu Athin does
an act and so infringes the law, and the Government
asks about it, I shall say, 'no'."

Source: As given by the Home Member, Su Maung Kin,
          in the Legislative Council on November 28,
          1923.   Quoted in Great Britain, India
          Office, Indian Constitutional Reforms,
          Views of Local Governments on the Working
          of the Reforms Dated 1927, p. 327.

APPENDIX E

EXTRACTS FROM AN OATH TAKEN BY

THE BURMESE REBELS, 1932

"Now at this time are we banded together to drive
out all unbelievers. . . . Till we are free from
the rule of the English we promise to harm no member of the Galon Society . . . so that our religion
may be saved from the unbeliever I will risk my
life . . . . Grant that I may help to destroy all
other unbelievers. . . . Protect and help our religion, O ye greater and lesser Nats. . . . Grant
to us liberty and to the Galon King dominion over
this land."

Source: C. V. Warren, <u>Burmese</u> <u>Interlude</u> (London,
          1937), pp. 92-94. This extract is from
          the oath obtained indirectly by Warren
          from Bo Hla Maung, an important rebel
          leader. The Galon is a mythical eagle
          adopted by the rebels as their symbol.
          The Galon King is Saya San, the leader of
          the rebellion. Nats are the animistic
          spirits of Burman folklore and religion.

APPENDIX F

NONAGRICULTURAL COOPERATIVE SOCIETIES

Number of Members of Nonagricultural Cooperative Societies

Activity	1919	1920	1921	1922	1923	1924
Purchases & Sales	152	389	718	1079	1053	1147
Production						92
Production & Sales			704	825	598	600

Activity	1925	1926	1927	1928	1929	1930
Purchases & Sales	1099	1261	389	540	541	777
Production	152	156	157	165	160	122
Production & Sales	903	1006	596	869	358	270

Activity	1931	1932	1933	1934	1935	1936
Purchases & Sales	844	897	772	1219	1344	1419
Production	118	120	116	116	116	107
Production & Sales	175	42	42	64	88	93

	1937
Purchases & Sales	1686
Production	50
Production & Sales	142

APPENDIX F (continued)

Number of Nonagricultural Cooperative Societies

Activity	1919	1920	1921	1922	1923	1924
Purchases & Sales	7	12	14	21	9	9
Production						2
Production & Sales			10	15	11	11

Activity	1925	1926	1927	1928	1929	1930
Purchases & Sales	8	6	7	7	5	5
Production	3	3	3	3	3	2
Production & Sales	13	15	15	18	15	13

Activity	1931	1932	1933	1934	1935	1936	1937
Purchases & Sales	5	7	6	7	7	7	9
Production	2	2	2	2	2	2	0
Production & Sales	10	2	2	4	4	4	3

Source: Burma, Financial Commissioner, Report on the Working of Cooperative Societies in Burma, Annual.

NOTES

1. In this study, the noun "Burmese" is used for the majority ethnic group in Burma.

2. (1) 1826, the eastern and western coastal provinces of Tenasserim and Arakan; (2) 1852, the central coastal provinces of Pegu and Martaban; (3) 1886, Upper Burma. See A. C. Banerjee, Annexation of Burma (Calcutta, 1944).

3. Policy statement by Sir Edwin Montagu, Secretary of State for India, August 20, 1917. Great Britain, Parliamentary Debates (House of Commons), Volume 97 (1917), Col. 1695-1696.

4. John S. Furnivall, Colonial Policy and Practice (London, 1948), pp. 49, 54.

5. Furnivall, op. cit., pp. 27-29, 42. John F. Cady, Patricia C. Barnett, and Shirley Jenkins, The Development of Self-Rule and Independence in Burma, Malaya and the Philippines (New York, 1948), p. 25. Burmese customary local government persisted until 1886. Furnivall, op. cit., p. 42.

6. Cambridge History of India (Cambridge, 1929), Volume V, pp. 567-568. Furnivall, op. cit., pp. 33-35. So heavily did concern for a nondeficit administration weigh in the policies of the Indian government that serious consideration was given in 1831 to a proposal to restore the newly won eastern coastal province of Tenasserim to Burma since its revenues were not meeting administrative expenses. W. S. Desai, History of the British Residency in Burma 1828-40 (Rangoon, 1939), pp. 57, 62, 132-137.

7. Furnivall, op. cit., pp. 48, 50, 78.

8. Cambridge History of India, Volume VI, p. 444.

9. Ma Mya Sein, The Administration of Burma (Rangoon, 1938), pp. 81-85, Chapter VII, IX. Furnivall, op. cit., pp. 73-77, 105-109. United States, Office of Strategic Services, The Problem of Law and Order in Burma under British Administration, Research and Analysis Report, 1944, pp. 30-36. Cambridge History of India, Volume VI, p. 442. G. Appleton, "The Burmese Viewpoint," Asiatic Review, Volume 44 (1948), pp. 233-251.

10. The 1897 Legislative Council consisted of

nine appointed members, five of whom were officials.
In 1909, the Council was enlarged to fifteen mem-
bers, with one of nine nonofficial members elected
by the European Chamber of Commerce. A. Ireland,
The Province of Burma, 2 vols. (Boston, 1907),
Volume I: 99-100. Furnivall, op. cit., pp. 71-72.

11. This move was carried out despite determined opposition from the timber companies.
Cambridge History of India, Volume V, p. 444.

12. Furnivall, op. cit., p. 64.

13. Ibid., pp. 41, 124-127.

14. These councils, concerned chiefly with
the needs of the European community for public
works, hospitals, and schools, did not have much
connection with Burmese society. Their efficiency
was largely a function of the energy of their
officials. F. B. Leach, The Future of Burma
(Rangoon, 1936), p. 95.

15. Furnivall, op. cit., p. 73.

16. Leach, op. cit., p. 71.

17. Furnivall, op. cit., pp. 99-100.

18. Burma, Crime Enquiry Committee, Report,
1923.

19. Sir Charles Crosthwaite, The Pacification
of Burma (London, 1912), passim.

20. Guy Wint, The British in Asia (London,
1947), p. 96. Mya Sein, op. cit., p. 158.

21. Mya Sein, op. cit., pp. 156-158. British
officials with long field experience in Burma at
times opposed administrative changes imposed from
above. See, for example, John F. Cady, A History
of Modern Burma (Ithaca, New York, 1958), p. 144.

22. Furnivall, op. cit., pp. 109-116.

NOTES FOR CHAPTER 2

1. Nationalism, in terms of ethnic and cultural identity, was deeply rooted in the history
and traditions of the Burmese. See Donald Eugene

214

Smith, <u>Religion</u> <u>and</u> <u>Politics</u> <u>in</u> <u>Burma</u> (Princeton, N.J., 1965), pp. 81-84. The term "nationalism" as used in this work, refers to the modern nationalist movement in pursuit of self-government and, eventually, independence.

2. Rupert Emerson, Lennox A. Mills, and Virginia Thompson, <u>Government</u> <u>and</u> <u>Nationalism</u> <u>in</u> <u>Southeast</u> <u>Asia</u> (New York, 1942), p. 25. H. G. Quaritch Wales, <u>Years</u> <u>of</u> <u>Blindness</u> (New York, 1943), p. 93. As Cady points out, following the first stirrings of the nationalist movement, it was the less Westernized Burmese who provided much of the popular political leadership.

3. Rupert Emerson, "An Analysis of Nationalism in Southeast Asia," <u>Far</u> <u>Eastern</u> <u>Quarterly</u> Volume 4 (1946), p. 208 ff.

4. Rupert Emerson, et al., <u>Government</u> <u>and</u> <u>Nationalism</u> <u>in</u> <u>Southeast</u> <u>Asia,</u> p. 5.

5. Furnivall, <u>op</u>. <u>cit</u>., p. 142. Leach, <u>op</u>. <u>cit</u>., p. 19. Burmese nationalists visited Japan just prior to World War II. Burma, Information Office, <u>Burma</u> <u>Handbook</u> (Simla, 1943), pp. 113-114. The Buddhism of Burma is of the Theravada school, differing in doctrine from the Mahayana form of Japan.

6. U.S. Consul, Rangoon, to the Department of State, October 20, 1931. Manuscript, Department of State, File 845.00/737. Hereafter reports from U.S. Consul, Rangoon, will be cited: From American Consul Rangoon, Date, Ms. D/S File ____. W. H. Graham, "Burmese Aspirations," <u>Asiatic</u> <u>Review,</u> Volume 26 (1920), p. 360.

7. Laymen's Foreign Mission Inquiry, <u>Fact</u> <u>Finders</u> <u>Report,</u> Volume 4, Part 2 (New York, 1933), p. 618.

8. Great Britain, India Office, <u>Addresses</u> <u>Presented</u> <u>in</u> <u>India</u> <u>to</u> <u>the</u> <u>Viceroy</u> <u>and</u> <u>Secretary</u> <u>of</u> <u>State,</u> Cd. 9178 (1918), p. 32. This official source notes that YMBA included many of the better educated and more progressive Burmese. N. C. Sen, <u>A</u> <u>Peep</u> <u>into</u> <u>Burma</u> <u>Politics</u> (Allahabad, India, 1945), pp. 7-8. Leach, <u>op</u>. <u>cit</u>., p. 33. Furnivall, <u>op</u>. <u>cit</u>., p. 143.

9. The only plotting involving peoples of Burma concerned some inconsequential affairs by

petty tribal chiefs. The Indian intrigue involved mainly Muslim secret societies in Rangoon in 1915 and an attempt to subvert the 130th Baluchi Regiment and the Military Police. German agents were involved. India, Sedition Committee, Revolutionary Conspiracies in India, Cd. 9190 (1919), pp. 70-72. William Roy Smith, Nationalism and Reform in India (New Haven, Conn., 1938), p. 81.

10. Burma Gazette (Supplement), 1916, pp. 759.

11. Burma, Education Department, Report of the Committee Appointed to Ascertain and Advise How the Imperial Idea May Be Inculcated and Fostered in Schools and Colleges in Burma, p. 10.

12. Ibid., p. 52. A Standing Committee on the Imperial Idea was maintained until the close of the war. Ibid., p. 53. The Standing Committee undertook to run the Boy Scout program, to improve the public relations of the schools, and to organize public lectures. Burma Gazette, Part IV (1918), pp. 453-456, 1171-1176.

13. Burma Gazette (Supplement), Nov. 1, 1919, p. 1120.

14. Ibid., pp. 119-1125. The government decided to allow the pongyis of each pagoda to decide the shoe question individually. The issue persisted for some time thereafter, and the Europeans generally acceded to the Burmese custom. Furnivall, op. cit., p. 143. The U.S. Consul in Rangoon mentioned the pagoda footwear controversy as the only case of an aggressive tendency among the Burmese. From American Consul, Rangoon, Sept. 11, 1918, Ms. D/S File 845.00/222.

15. Great Britain, Parliamentary Debates (House of Commons), 5th ser., Volume 97 (1917), Col. 1695-1696.

16. From American Consul, Rangoon, Sept. 11, 1918, Ms. D/S File 845.00/222.

17. Sir Reginald Craddock, The Dilemma in India (London, 1930), p. 109.

18. Ibid. Great Britain, India Office, Letter from the Government of India to the Secretary of State and Enclosures, Cmd. 123 (1918), p. 250.

19. Great Britain, India Office, Addresses

Presented in India to the Viceroy and Secretary
of State for India, Cd. 9178 (1918), p. 32. The
deputation included U Phay, a retired official, U
May Oung, prominent in the early YMBA, U Ba Pe,
later to lead the Nationalist Party, and U Su,
of the YMBA. Great Britain, Indian Statutory Commission, Volume XVII, Selections from Memoranda and
Oral Evidence by Non-Officials, p. 395.

20. Great Britain, Indian Statutory Commission, Volume XI, Memorandum Submitted by the Government of Burma, p. 7.

21. Great Britain, India Office, Proposals
of the Government of India for a New Constitution
for Burma, Cmd. 746 (1919), p. 30.

22. Leach, op. cit., p. 33. Sen, op. cit.,
p. 36. Craddock maintained that the Younger Party
was supported by Indian interests. Craddock, op.
cit., p. 116. The Burma government maintained that
the Younger Party was not the voice of the people
and was seeking to gain the aid of the Indian
National Congress to achieve their ends. Great
Britain, India Office, Proposals of the Government
of India for a New Constitution for Burma, Cmd. 746
(1919), p. 30.

23. Great Britain, Indian Statutory Commission, Volume XVII, Selections from Memoranda and
Oral Evidence by Non-Officials, p. 396. Pamphlets
were printed in Britain pleading Burma's cause. A
newspaper advertisement "Burma's Appeal to Britain"
appeared in October, 1919, claiming the right of
self-determination. See the London Daily News,
October 31, 1919, p. 7.

24. Great Britain, Parliament, Joint Committee
on the Government of India Bill, Report, Proceedings, Evidence, Appendices, /Sessional Papers, 1919,
Volume IV, Report (203)/, p. 138. U Pu claimed
the Burma Reform League had 10,000 members in 220
associations.

25. Great Britain, India Office, Correspondence on Burma Reforms, Cmd. 1194 (1921), p. 9.

26. Ibid.

27. Burma, Police Department, Report on the
Police Administration in Burma, 1919, p. 35.

28. Burma, Police Department, Report on the

<u>Police</u> <u>Administration</u> <u>in</u> <u>Burma,</u> 1920, p. 311. The
staff of the Criminal Investigation Department was
increased accordingly.

29. Great Britain, Indian Statutory Commis-
sion, Volume XI, <u>Memorandum</u> <u>Submitted</u> <u>by</u> <u>The</u> <u>Govern-
ment</u> <u>of</u> <u>Burma,</u> pp. 25, 267. Great Britain, <u>Parlia-
mentary</u> <u>Debates</u> (House of Commons), Volume 134
(1920), Col. 1899. The election boycott was also
in response to Indian efforts to gain the cooperation of Burma's political leaders in an India-wide
boycott of the elections. John F. Cady, <u>A</u> <u>History</u>
<u>of</u> <u>Modern</u> <u>Burma,</u> p. 216.

30. The anniversary of the university boycott
was designated National Day in Burma. Great Britain, Indian Statutory Commission, Volume XI,
<u>Memorandum</u> <u>Submitted</u> <u>by</u> <u>the</u> <u>Government</u> <u>of</u> <u>Burma,</u>
p. 25. <u>Burma</u> <u>Gazette</u> (Supplement), 1920, p. 1317.
Sen, <u>op</u>. <u>cit</u>., pp. 8-12.

31. John L. Christian, <u>Burma</u> <u>and</u> <u>the</u> <u>Japanese</u>
<u>Invader</u> (Bombay, 1945), p. 238. Sen, op. cit., p.
25. Burma, Police Department, <u>Report</u> <u>on</u> <u>the</u> <u>Police</u>
<u>Administration</u> <u>in</u> <u>Burma,</u> 1921, p. 9.

32. <u>Burma</u> <u>Gazette</u> (Part I), 1921, p. 28.

33. <u>Burma</u> <u>Gazette</u> (Part III), 1921, p. 28.

34. Great Britain, Indian Statutory Commis-
sion, Volume XI, <u>Memorandum</u> <u>Submitted</u> <u>by</u> <u>the</u> <u>Govern-
ment</u> of Burma, p. 25. Craddock, <u>op</u>. <u>cit</u>., p. 18.
"Home rule" presumably meant local autonomy in all
fields of government except foreign relations and
defense.

35. Sen, <u>op</u>. <u>cit</u>., pp. 14-15.

36. <u>Indian</u> <u>Daily</u> <u>News</u> (Calcutta), July 5,
1921.

37. Ibid., July 7, 1921. Great Britain, Indian Statutory Commission, Volume XI, <u>Memorandum</u>
<u>Submitted</u> <u>by</u> <u>the</u> <u>Government</u> <u>of</u> <u>Burma,</u> pp. 25, 267.

38. Great Britain, Burma Reform Committee,
<u>Report,</u> p. 5. U Myint who served on the committee
stated that he was not subject to insult or intimidation. <u>Burma</u> <u>Gazette</u> (Part III), 1922, p. 8.

39. <u>Times</u> (London), May 24, 1922. Great
Britain, Indian Statutory Commission, Volume XI,

Government of Burma Memorandum, pp. 25, 268.
Burma Gazette, Part III, 1921, p. 340; Part III,
1922, pp. 8, 13. The government stated that seven
leaders had been interned including U Chit Hlaing.
Ibid., p. 12. Craddock, op. cit., p. 119. However,
a Burmese theatrical troupe who performed for the
prince was subsequently attacked by pongyis at a
pagoda festival. Donald Eugene Smith, op. cit.,
p. 105.

40.   Burma, Police Department, Report on the
Police Administration in Burma, 1924, p. 18.

41.   The Police Commissioner, North-West
Border, believed that "Nationalism is merely the
substitution of wider ideals and a conception of
the advantages of cooperation, and the athins must
study to keep these points constantly in view, if
they are to help the country." Burma, Police
Department, Report on the Police Administration in
Burma, 1922, p. 18. Many of the officials considered the athins a hindrance to the police, however.
Ostensibly at least athins were set up to suppress
vice and crime. Paul Edmonds, Peacocks and Pagodas
(London, 1924), p. 131.

42.   Burma Gazette, Part III, 1922, pp. 41 ff.

43.   Ibid.

44.   Ibid., pp. 220, 263. By 1927 the government had sanctioned prosecutions against 124 athins.
This figure does not include prosecutions of individuals as such. Great Britain, India Office, Views
of the Local Governments on the Working of the
Reforms, 1927, p. 415.

45.   Great Britain, Indian Statutory Commission, Volume XI, Memorandum Submitted by the Government of Burma, p. 268.

46.   U Chit Hlaing, who had been the president
of first the YMBA and then the GCBA since 1918,
Tharrawaddy U Pu and U Tun Aung Gyaw. This group
was closely associated with the political pongyi,
U Ottama. Sen, op. cit., p. 17. See also Burma
Round Table Conference, London 1931-1932, Proceed-
ings, Cmd. 4004 (1932), pp. 71-73 for Tharrawaddy
U Pu's account of the split. Burma, Information
Office, Burma Handbook, p. 106. Furnivall, op.
cit., pp. 43-44. Leach, op. cit., p. 34. Great
Britain, India Office, Views of Local Governments
on the Working of the Reforms, 1927, p. 325.

47. Great Britain, India Office, <u>Views of
Local Governments on the Working of the Reforms,
1927,</u> p. 325. Great Britain, Indian Statutory Commission, Volume XI, <u>Memorandum Submitted by the
Government of Burma,</u> pp. 349, 356.

48. Ibid., p. 268.

49. Great Britain, Reforms Enquiry Committee,
<u>Views of the Local Governments on the Working of
Reforms, 1924.</u> Cmd. 2362 (1924), p. 61. Sen, <u>op.
cit.</u>, pp. 17-18. Great Britain, Indian Statutory
Commission, Volume XI, <u>Memorandum Submitted by the
Government of Burma,</u> pp. 39, 268, 273.

50. <u>Burma Gazette</u> (Extraordinary), Dec. 15,
1923, p. 1. Great Britain, Indian Statutory Commission, Volume XV, <u>Extracts from Official Oral
Evidence,</u> p. 459. The budget cut was largely in the
funds for the Criminal Intelligence Division. From
the American Consul, Rangoon, Dec. 25, 1923, Ms.
D/S File 845.00/426.

51. Great Britain, Indian Statutory Commission, Volume XI, <u>Memorandum Submitted by the
Government of Burma,</u> pp. 638-669.

52. Ibid., p. 356; <u>Times</u> (London), Aug. 29,
1924, p. 9; <u>Forward</u> (Calcutta), Aug. 24, 1924,
p. 3; Aug. 29, 1924, p. 5.

53. The committee held that crime was not
associated with the land tenure system. Burma,
Crime Enquiry Committee, <u>Report of the Crime
Enquiry Committee.</u>

54. <u>Burma Gazette</u>, Part III, 1922, p. 13;
1920, pp. 109, 110, 121.

55. Furnivall, <u>op. cit.</u>, pp. 199-201. Craddock, <u>op. cit.</u>, p. 117. Sen, <u>op. cit.</u>, pp. 15-16.

56. Great Britain, Indian Statutory Commission, Volume XI, <u>Memorandum Submitted by the Government of Burma</u>, p. 25. The GCSS split as did the
GCBA. The corresponding sections of each joined
forces although there was often jealousy between
the monks and the laymen. Leach, <u>op. cit.</u>, p. 34.

57. The courts set aside a conviction for
defamation in this case. Nga On Thin and Seventy
Others vs. King Emperor I, <u>Burma Law Journal</u>
(1922), p. 39.

58. *Burma* *Gazette,* Part III, 1922, p. 13.

59. Burma, Police Department, *Report* *on* *the* *Police* *Administration* *in* *Burma,* *1922,* p. 16. Great Britain, Reforms Enquiry Committee, *Views* *of* *the* *Local* *Governments* *on* *the* *Working* *of* *the* *Reforms,* *1924,* p. 14.

60. *Forward* (Calcutta), Jul. 30, 1924, p. 5; Aug. 2, 1924, p. 9.

61. Ibid.

62. *Indian* *Law* *Reports,* Rangoon Series, p. 211.

63. *Bu* *athin* derived its name from the Burmese *mathibu* meaning "I do not know." From the American Consul, Rangoon, Aug. 22, 1923, Ms. D/S File 845.00/399. For the origin of one *bu* *athin,* see F. Bigg-Wither "Cleaning Up Burma's Murder Zone," *Contemporary* *Review* Volume 56 (1939), pp. 715-722. For the *Bu* *Athin* oath, see Appendix D.

64. Burma, Police Department, *Report* *on* *Police* *Administration* *in* *Burma,* *1923,* p. 38.

65. *Burma* *Gazette,* Part I, 1923, p. 966. Fifty-seven *bu* *athins* in the delta area were declared unlawful by this first order. Great Britain, India Office, *Views* *of* *Local* *Governments* *on* *the* *Working* *of* *the* *Reforms,* *1927,* p. 415.

66. *Burma* *Gazette,* Part I, 1924, p. 763.

67. For example, *Burma* *Gazette,* Part I, 1923,

68. Burma, *Report* *on* *the* *Administration* *of* Burma *1925-6,* p. 22. Edmonds, *op.* *cit.,* p. 31.

69. Great Britain, Indian Statutory Commission, Volume XI, *Memorandum* *Submitted* *by* *the* *Government* *of* *Burma,* p. 216. Burma, Police Department, *Report* *on* *the* *Police* *Administration* *of* *Burma,* *1924,* p. 12. Special gun and cattle *athins* were formed to protect villages from dacoits. *Burma* *Gazette,* Supplement, 1924, p. 184.

70. A Tikoka and Ba Sein vs. King Emperor I; *Indian* *Law* *Reports,* Rangoon Series, p. 629. See also King Emperor vs. Nga Aung Gyau et al.; Ibid., p. 604.

71. Burma, Report on the Administration of B
Burma 1923-4, p. 24.

72. Furnivall, op. cit., p. 195. Great Britain, Indian Statutory Commission, Volume XI,
Memorandum Submitted by the Government of Burma,
p. 314. The Village Committees were legally constituted in the Rural Self-Government Act of 1921
but were never activated until after 1924. Ibid.,
p. 947.

73. Thus in 1925 a group of dacoits declared
they were Wunthanu dacoits and would pillage only
foreigners. Burma, Police Department, Report on
the Police Administration in Burma, 1925, p. 34.

74. Burma Gazette, Supplement, 1925, pp. 170-
201. Burma, Police Department, Report on the
Police Administration in Burma, 1923, p. 26; 1925,
p. 31; 1921, p. 13. Of 2096 murders in Burma
during 1924, 1925, and the first half of 1926,
thirteen were attributed to "politics." Burma
Gazette, Supplement, 1926, p. 804.

75. The capitation tax was levied on all male
adults in Lower Burma in addition to land revenue.
Married men paid Rs. 5 per annum, unmarried Rs. 2.5.
Great Britain, Indian Statutory Commission, Volume
XI, Memorandum Submitted by the Government of Burma,
pp. 166, 26. Burma, Police Department, Report on
the Police Administration in Burma, 1924, p. 12.
Great Britain, India Office, Views of Local Govern-
ments on the Working of the Reforms, 1927, p. 326.
The rupee was valued at $0.36.

76. Ibid.

77. Ibid. Times (London), Oct. 17, 1924,
p. 13. U Chit Hlaing contended to the contrary.
Burma Round Table Conference, London 1931-1932,
Proceedings, p. 100.

78. Burma, Financial Commissioner, Report on
the Land Revenue Administration, 1925, p. 26.

79. Great Britain, Indian Statutory Commission, Volume XI, Memorandum Submitted by the Government of Burma, pp. 171-172.

NOTES FOR CHAPTER 3

1. Rangoon <u>Mail,</u> May 11, 1924. Great Britain, Indian Statutory Commission, Volume XI, <u>Memorandum Submitted by the Government of Burma,</u> pp. 171-172. The <u>Police Administration Report 1924</u> placed the Paungde Conference attendance at 30,000 (p. 49). The GCBA, claiming 7,000 member associations, asserted 150,000 were present. <u>Forward</u> (Calcutta), Aug. 19, 1924, p. 10.

2. Burma, Police Department, <u>Report</u> on <u>Police Administration in Burma 1924,</u> pp. 13, 48. For U Ottama's version of the affair see his telegram to the Viceroy. <u>Forward</u> (Calcutta), Aug. 21, 1924, p. 3. He contended that the Union Party was a puppet group working to separate Burma from India.

3. <u>Times</u> (London), Oct. 6, 1924; Oct. 10, 1924.

4. Sen, <u>op. cit.</u>, p. 27. From American Consul, Rangoon, Nov. 26, 1925, Ms. D/S File 845.00/ 499. Great Britain, India Office, <u>Reports of the Local Governments on the Working of the Reforms, 1927,</u> p. 60. Great Britain, Indian Statutory Commission, Volume XI, <u>Memorandum Submitted by the Government of Burma,</u> pp. 265, 269-271.

5. Ibid., pp. 30, 271-274, 337, 361-367. Sen, <u>op. cit.</u>, p. 27. <u>Times</u> (London), Mar. 8, 1926, p. 3; Mar. 13, 1926, p. 11.

6. Burma, Police Department, <u>Report on the Police Administration in Burma, 1927,</u> p. 67. Burma, <u>Report on the Administration of Burma 1927-28,</u> p. 23. Maurice Collis, <u>Trials in Burma,</u> pp. 34-35. Great Britain, Indian Statutory Commission, Volume XI, <u>Memorandum Submitted by the Government of Burma,</u> p. 25.

7. The Burma for Burmans League associated itself with this draft based on the constitution of the Irish Free State. Ibid., pp. 385, 407-408; Burma, <u>Report on the Administration of Burma 1928-9,</u> pp. x-xi.

8. Great Britain, Indian Statutory Commission, Volume XVII, <u>Selections from Memoranda and Oral Evidence by Non-Officials,</u> p. 409. Burma, <u>Report on the Administration of Burma 1928-29,</u> p. xi. <u>Times</u> (London), Nov. 15, 1928, p. 15. Sen, <u>op. cit.</u>, pp. 29-32. Sen confuses the sequence of

223

events in this period.

9. India, Legislature, Legislative Assembly, Debates (1929), Volume V, pp. 1396-1418. Burma, Report on the Administration of Burma 1929-30, p. xii. Sen, op. cit., p. 32.

10. Great Britain, Indian Statutory Commission, Volume XVII, Selections from Memoranda and Official Oral Evidence, p. 393. Burma, Report on the Administration of Burma 1928-29, p. xi. Collis, op. cit., pp. 41-46. Forward (Calcutta), Jan. 30, 1929; Jan. 31, 1929.

11. See below p. 82.

12. Burma, Report on the Administration of Burma, 1929-30, p. xii. Burma, Riots Inquiry Commission, Interim Report, p. 43.

13. Burmese tradition looked to the revival of the Burmese Buddhist monarchy. For an analysis of the folk beliefs, which played a major part in the Saya San uprising, see E. Sarkisyanz, Buddhist Background of the Burmese Rebellion (The Hague, 1965), pp. 149-165. Collis, op. cit., pp. 208-210, gives a description of the ceremony and tradition utilized by Saya San who was reputed to be of royal descent.

14. The rebels took an oath pledging them to drive the "Unbelievers" out of Burma. See Appendix E. For the text of Saya San's "declaration of war" see Liberty (Calcutta), Jan. 13, 1931.

15. By December 28th the rebel force was estimated to consist of 1,200-1,500 men. Thirty guns, one or two rifles, and considerable ammunition had been seized by the rebels. Great Britain, India Office, Report on the Rebellion in Burma up to 3rd May, 1931, Cmd. 3900 (1931), p. 3.

16. Great Britain, Parliamentary Debates (House of Commons), Volume 254 (1931), Col. 2310.

17. Ibid., Col. 2311. The government forces killed or wounded some 3,000 persons in quelling the revolt. About 50 of the government forces, including officials, were killed. Godfrey Eric Harvey, British Rule in Burma, 1824-1942 (London, 1946), pp. 73, 74.

18. Mi Mi Khaing, Burmese Family (Bombay,

1946), p. 94.

19. United States, Office of Strategic Services, The Problem of Law and Order in Burma under British Administration (Research and Analysis Report 1980) (Washington, 1944), pp. 86-87.

20. See below, p. 91.

21. Burma, Report on the Administration of Burma, 1931-32, p. viii. Cady, A History of Modern Burma, pp. 301-302, 336-337.

22. Ibid., p. 339.

23. Sen, op. cit., p. 47.

24. Ibid., pp. 48-49. Great Britain, Parliamentary Debates (House of Lords), Volume 96 (1932), Cols. 975-978.

25. The Joint Committees Report stated, "The inference we draw from our examination of the course pursued by the Burman Anti-Separationists is that, in fact, they desire the separation of their country from India, but are distrustful of the consequences which may follow if the step is taken now." Great Britain, Parliament, House of Commons, Sessional Papers, Vol. VI for 1933-34, "Report of the Joint Committee on Indian Constitutional Reform" (London, 1934), Pt. I, Sec. 6, "Burma," p. 249.

26. The Burma Police were probably more concerned about a communist overflow from India than any activities of the few poorly organized Burmese who had been exposed to Marxist writings. Burma, Police Department, Report on the Police Administration in Burma 1933, p. 43.

27. Walter D. Sutton, Jr., "U Aung San of Burma," South Atlantic Quarterly 47 (Jan., 1948): 1-16.

28. Christian, op. cit., p. 187.

29. Ibid., p. 247. U Ba Maw, Breakthrough in Burma (New Haven, 1968), p. 15.

30. Burma, Information Office, Burma Handbook, p. 106.

NOTES FOR CHAPTER 4

1. Rupert Emerson, et al., Government and Nationalism in Southeast Asia, p. 159.

2. Ganga Singh, Burma Parliamentary Companion, pp. 37-38. Furnivall, op. cit., pp. 71-72.

3. Montagu's original draft called for "free institutions" and "ultimate self-government." Lawrence John L. Dundas, Earl of Ronaldshay, Life of Lord Curzon (London, 1928), Volume III, p. 167.

4. Ibid., pp. 103, 105. Montagu's dairy offers no explanation for this shift in plans. Edwin S. Montagu, An Indian Dairy, edited by Venetia Montagu (London, 1930). Possibly Montagu concluded that his proposal for a separate Burma under the Viceroy would not be regarded as adequate by the government of Burma or the Burmese advocates of separation. See Cady, A History of Modern Burma, p. 201.

5. Great Britain, India Office, Report on Indian Constitutional Reforms, Cd. 9109 (1918), pp. 156, 162.

6. Burma Gazette, Part III, 1919, p. 82.

7. Ibid. Great Britain, India Office, Proposals of the Government of India for a New Constititution for Burma, Cmd. 746 (1920), p. 76.

8. Ibid. The governors of the major provinces including Burma in a joint minute proposed to associate Indians in the government as a "bridge" to popular rule. Great Britain, India Office, Letter from the Government of India to the Secretary of State and Enclosures, Cmd. 123 (1919), p. 41.

9. Great Britain, Indian Statutory Commission, Volume XVII, Selections from Memoranda and Oral Evidence by Non-Officials, p. 395. Great Britain, Parliament Joint Committee on the Government of India Bill, Report, Proceedings, Evidence, Appendices (Sessional Papers, 1919, Report) (203), Volume 1, p. 299.

10. Ibid., p. 11.

11. Great Britain, Parliamentary Debates

(House of Commons), Volume 122 (1919), Col. 491-494.

12. Ibid., Volume 129 (1920), Col. 1432-1433.

13. Great Britain, Indian Statutory Commission, Volume XVII, Selections from Memoranda and Oral Evidence by Non-Officials, p. 402.

14. Great Britain, Parliamentary Debates (House of Commons), Volume 136 (1920), Col. 140.

15. Great Britain, India Office, Report of the Committee on Financial Relations, Cmd. 724 (1920), p. 28.

16. Great Britain, Indian Statutory Commission, Reports of the Committee Appointed by the Provincial Legislative Councils to Cooperate with the Indian Statutory Commission, Cmd. 3572 (1930), p. 511.

17. Burma Gazette, Part III, 1921, pp. 28-33. Great Britain, India Office, Correspondence on Burma Reforms, Cmd. 1194 (1921), p. 61.

18. Great Britain, Parliament, Standing Joint Committee on Indian Affairs, Second Report of the Committee (Sessional Papers, 1921, Volume VI, Report 203), p. 114.

19. Great Britain, Burma Reforms Committee, Report, p. 1. The notification had established 60 percent as the minimum percentage of elected members in the governor's Legislative Council of 92. Burma Gazette, Part I, 1921, p. 701.

20. Great Britain, Burma Reforms Committee, Report, Appendix IV, pp. 36-47.

21. Great Britain, Parliamentary Debates (House of Commons), Volume 155 (1922), Vol. 51-156; (House of Lords), Volume 51 (1922), Col. 79-87.

22. Burma Gazette (Extraordinary), Jan. 2, 1923.

23. Great Britain, Indian Statutory Commission, Volume XI, Memorandum Submitted by the Government of Burma, pp. 28-33. Furnivall, op. cit., pp. 159-160.

24. Ibid., pp. 277-278.

25. From American Consul, Rangoon, Nov. 26, 1925, Ms. D/S File 845.00/499.

26. From American Consul, Rangoon, Nov. 1, 1924, Ms. D/S File 845.00/437. Forward (Calcutta), Aug. 24, 1924; Aug. 29, 1924.

27. India, Indian Central Committee, Report of the Indian Central Committee 1928-29, Cmd. 3451 (1929), pp. 27, 73-82.

28. Great Britain, Indian Statutory Commission, Volume III, Reports of the Committees Appointed by the Provincial Legislative Councils to Cooperate with the Indian Statutory Commission, Cmd. 3572 (1930), p. 510.

29. Ibid.

30. Great Britain, Indian Statutory Commission, Volume XI, Memorandum Submitted by the Government of Burma, p. 576.

31. Ibid., p. 583.

32. Great Britain, Indian Statutory Commission, Volume XVII, Selections from Memoranda and Oral Evidence by Non-Officials, pp. 359-466. The Karen National League admitted Dominion Home Rule "might be bloody rule, but blood often purifies rules, it at least simplifies them." Ibid., p. 424.

33. Ibid., pp. 400-409.

34. Great Britain, Indian Statutory Commission, Volume II, Recommendations, p. 190.

35. Indian Round Table Conference, London, 1930-1931, Proceedings, Cmd. 3778 (1931), p. 197.

36. Ibid., p. 366.

37. Ibid., p. 503.

38. Burma Round Table Conference, London, 1931-1932, Proceedings of the Committee of the Whole Conference, p. 6.

39. Ibid., p. 75.

40. Ibid., p. 77. Tharrawaddy U Pu resumed participation two days after, on Dec. 16, 1931.

228

41. Great Britain, Parliament, Joint Committee on Indian Constitutional Reform. /Session 1933-1934/, Volume I, Part I, Report.

42. 26 Geo. 5, Ch. 3.

43. "Instrument of Instructions to the Governor of Burma," as found in Ganga Singh, Burma Parliamentary Companion, p. 152.

44. Government of Burma Act, 1935, Article 139. The Proclamation invoking this power was valid for six months subject to extension by the Parliament in London.

45. Maung Maung, Burma's Constitution, 2d ed. (The Hague, 1961), p. 30.

46. Cady, A History of Modern Burma, pp. 353-354.

NOTES FOR CHAPTER 5

1. See the Minute submitted by Governor Craddock of Burma and others Jan., 1919. Great Britain, India Office, Letter from the Government of India to the Secretary of State and Enclosures, Cmd. 1923 (1919), p. 36.

2. Speech by Governor Craddock in the Legislative Council, April 9, 1921. Burma Gazette, Part III, 1921, p. 156.

3. Great Britain, Royal Commission on the Superior Civil Services in India, Report of the Royal Commission on the Superior Civil Services in India, Cmd. 2128 (1924), p. 8.

4. Great Britain, Royal Commission on the Indian Public Services, Report of the Royal Commission on the Indian Public Services, Vol. XI, Appendices V, VII. The term Buddhist in this context seemingly refers predominately to Burmese. In 1927 the rupee was worth $0.36 at official rates.

5. Ibid., Volume IV, Appendix X.

6. Mya Sein, The Administration of Burma, pp. 91-92.

7. Great Britain, Indian Statutory Commission,

Volume XI, Memorandum Submitted by the Government of Burma, pp. 224-233.

8. Ibid., p. 227.

9. Great Britain, Royal Commission on the Superior Civil Services in India, Report of the Royal Commission on the Superior Civil Services in India, Cmd. 2128 (1924), p. 55.

10. Burma Gazette, Part II, 1920, p. 67.

11. Ibid.

12. Great Britain, Royal Commission on the Superior Civil Services in India, Report of the Royal Commission on the Superior Civil Services in India, Cmd. 2128 (1924), p. 55.

13. Ibid., p. 129.

14. Ibid.

15. Great Britain, Parliamentary Debates (House of Commons), Volume 262 (1932), Col. 787. These estimates were given by Sir Samuel Hoare, the Secretary of State for India. Anglo-Indians are not included.

16. Great Britain, Royal Commission on the Superior Civil Services in India, Report of the Royal Commission on the Superior Civil Services in India, p. 55. Great Britain, India Office, Proposals of the Government of India for a New Constitution of Burma, Cmd. 746 (1920), p. 10.

17. Leach, Future of Burma, p. 36.

18. Great Britain, Royal Commission on the Indian Public Services, Report of the Royal Commission on the Public Services in India, Volume IV, Appendix X, p. 138.

19. Great Britain, India Office, Report on Indian Constitutional Reforms, Cd. 9109 (1918), p. 162. The Royal Commission on the Superior Civil Services in India objected to the appointment of Indians to serve in the ICS in Burma. Report on the Superior Civil Services in India, Volume IV, Appendices, p. 138.

20. India, Census Commissioner, Census of India, 1931, Volume XI, Burma, Part II, pp. 192-193.

21. Great Britain, Indian Statutory Commission, Volume XI, Memorandum Submitted by the Government of Burma, p. 329.

22. Furnivall, op. cit., p. 175.

NOTES FOR CHAPTER 6

1. George Scott, Burma, A Handbook, p. 129.

2. D. J. Fleming, "The Church in Burma," in Laymans Foreign Mission Inquiry, Fact Finders Reports (New York, 1933), Volume IV, Part 2, p. 620. Cady, et al., The Development of Self-Rule and Independence in Burma, Malaya and the Philippines, p. 12.

3. Sir Harcourt Butler, Collection of Speeches (Rangoon, 1927), p. 154. Cady, et al., The Development of Self-Rule and Independence in Burma, Malaya and the Philippines, p. 16.

4. H. G. Quaritch Wales, Years of Blindness, p. 93.

5. Cady, et al., The Development of Self-Rule and Independence in Burma, Malaya and the Philippines, p. 40.

6. Great Britain, Indian Statutory Commission, Volume I, Survey, p. 78.

7. B. R. Pearn, The Indian in Burma (Racial Relations Studies in Conflict and Cooperation No. 4) (Ladbury, England), p. 20.

8. Burma, Police Department, Report on the Police Administration in Burma, 1920, p. 15.

9. "Report on the Disturbances in Rangoon during May 1930," Burma Gazette, Supplement, pp. 891-909.

10. Burma, Report on the Administration of Burma 1931-32, p. ix.

11. Burma, Report on the Administration of Burma 1930-31, p. 41.

12. B. R. Pearn, The Mixed Races of Burma (Racial Relations Studies in Conflict and Coopera-

tion No. 3) (Ladbury, England), p. 12.

13. Ibid. Cady, et al., The Development of Self-Rule and Independence in Burma, Malaya and the Philippines, pp. 12-13.

14. Christian, op. cit., p. 47.

15. Great Britain, Burma Reforms Committee, Report, p. 21.

16. Sen, op, cit., p. 23.

17. Great Britain, Parliament, Joint Committee on Indian Constitutional Reform /Session 1933-4/, Report, Proceedings and Records, 2 volumes, Volume II, Records, p. 19.

18. U Ba Pe even contended that minorities did not exist since no communal group comprised 20 percent of the population which was the criterion established by the League of Nations. Burma Round Table Conference, London, 1931-1932, Proceedings of the Committee of the Whole Conference, p. 30.

19. Great Britain, Indian Statutory Commission, Volume XVII, Selections from Memoranda and Oral Evidence by Non-Officials, p. 407.

20. Ibid., p. 418.

21. Great Britain, Parliament, Joint Committee on Indian Constitutional Reform /Session 1933-4/, Volume II, Records, p. 75.

22. David Graham Pole, India in Transition (London, 1934), p. 218.

23. Burmese nationalists spoke of "the enthusiastic cravings of their spirits for nationalism, their desire to be a nation, a distinct entity in the British Commonwealth, the natural longing of their individuality. . . ." Burma Gazette, Part III, 1921, p. 254.

24. Great Britain, Indian Statutory Commission, Volume I, Survey, p. 78.

25. India, Legislative Assembly, Debates, Volume III, Part I, 1922, p. 484.

26. Montagu, op. cit., p. 86.

27. James Baxter, Report on Indian Immigration (Rangoon, 1939), p. 97.

28. See below, pp. 172-175 for tariff controversy with India over rice control profits.

29. Great Britain, India Office, Report on Indian Constitutional Reforms, Cd. 9109 (1818), Paragraph 198.

30. Furnivall, op. cit., pp. 178-181.

31. Burma Gazette, Part III, 1919, p. 76.

32. India, Legislative Assembly, Debates, Volume VI, 1925, p. 781. Henry Craw, "Burma," Asiatic Review 38 (1943): 259-266.

33. Great Britain, India Office, Government of India's Despatches on Proposals for Constitutional Reform Dated 20th September, 1930, Cmd. 3700 (1930), p. 81.

34. Great Britain, Indian Statutory Commission, Volume II, Recommendations, p. 184.

35. Great Britain, Indian Statutory Commission, Volume XVII, Selections from Memoranda and Non-Official Oral Evidence, p. 392.

36. Great Britain, Parliament, Joint Committee on Indian Constitutional Reform /Session 1933-34/, Volume II, Records, p. 187.

37. Furnivall, op. cit., p. 184.

NOTES FOR CHAPTER 7

1. Burmese of the ahmudan class had been associated with the courts of the Burmese kings as retainers (atwintha) and as soldiers. See Cady, A History of Modern Burma, pp. 13-14, 36.

2. "Except in a small section of the population, public opinion cannot be said to exist." Great Britain, Indian Statutory Commission, Volume XI, Memorandum Submitted by the Government of Burma, p. 337.

3. Great Britain, India Office, Correspondence Regarding Report of the Committee, Cmd. 1671 (1922), p. 3.

4. The testimony of John S. Furnivall before the Burma Reforms Committee was particularly trenchant. He felt that the wide franchise proposed by the government was "certain to entail disaster" and favored granting use of the ballot only to those who actively sought the privilege. Great Britain, Burma Reforms Committee, Report, p. 63. Evidence, Volume I, pp. 40-49. Evidence, Volume III, pp. 216-233.

5. Great Britain, Burma Reforms Committee, Report, p. 55.

6. Great Britain, Indian Statutory Commission, Volume XI, Memorandum Submitted by the Government of Burma, p. 249.

7. Great Britain, Indian Statutory Commission, Volume XV, Extracts from Official Oral Evidence, p. 438.

8. An increase in the number of polling stations was in part responsible for the increased vote in 1925. Great Britain, Indian Statutory Commission, Volume XI, Memorandum Submitted by the Government of Burma, p. 256.

9. Great Britain, Indian Statutory Commission, Volume XV, Extracts from Official Oral Evidence, p. 437.

10. Tharrawaddy U Pu proposed a seven-year period of residence in Burma to establish eligibility for voting. Burma Round Table Conference, London 1931-1932, Proceedings of the Committee of the Whole Conference, p. 203.

11. Government of Burma Act 1935, Chapter III.

12. Cady, et al., The Development of Self-Rule and Independence in Burma, Malaya and the Philippines, p. 8. Limited government support was given to the Anglican church in Burma, mainly to provide religious facilities for British troops. Ecclesiastical affairs was a reserved subject.

13. India, A Collection of Acts Passed by the Governor General in Council, Act XI of 1919.

14. Burma, Report on the Administration of Burma, 1918-19, p. 21.

15. Burma, Report on the Administration of

Burma, 1921-22, p. 16.

16. India, A Collection of the Acts of the Indian Legislature and of the Governor General, 1924, Act VI of 1924.

17. Burma Gazette, Part II, 1922, p. 11.

18. Great Britain, India Office, Proposals of the Government of India for a New Constitution for Burma, Cmd. 746 (1920), p. 41.

19. During consideration of the Burma Rural Self Government Bill in 1921 the government spokesman in the Legislative Council advanced the opinion that "The criterion by which ten years hence the Province of Burma will be judged fit for a larger instalment of self-government will very probably be the extent to which the inhabitants of this country have made use of the powers of self-government which it is proposed to confer on them by the Rural Self Government Bill." Burma Gazette, Part III, 1921, p. 168.

20. Burmese nationalists maintained that "Training in Local Government is not training in Self-Government; the former, in short, is administration, whereas the latter is legislation and decision of great questions of policy." Statement by U Mya U, All Burma Mass Meeting, Aug. 26, 1928. Great Britain, Indian Statutory Commission, Volume XVII, Selections from Memoranda and Non-Official Oral Evidence, p. 397.

21. Furnivall, op. cit., p. 53.

22. Burma Gazette, Supplement, 1925, p. 20.

23. Source: Burma, Report on the Working of the District Councils 1925-26, p. 7.

24. The Burma government maintained that the thugyis were only "quasi-officials," Burma Gazette, Part III, 1921, p. 281.

25. Burma Gazette, Supplement, 1927, p. 382.

26. Burma Gazette, Supplement, 1927, p. 1159.

27. Burma, Review of the District Councils 1923-24, p. 8.

28. Of sixteen District Council accounts re-

235

ported on in 1927, eight were unsatisfactory and four very unsatisfactory. *Burma Gazette*, Supplement, 1927.

29. *Burma Gazette*, Part III, 1922, p. 409.

30. Great Britain, Indian Statutory Commission, Volume XVII, *Selections from Memoranda and Non-Official Oral Evidence*, p. 226.

31. Leach, *op. cit.*, p. 95.

32. Source: Burma, *Resolutions Reviewing the Report on the Working of Municipal Committees in Burma (Except Rangoon)*, 1917-18 and 1918-19, 1920-21.

33. Ibid., 1920-21.

34. Source: Burma, *Review of Municipal Administration (Except Rangoon) 1928*.

35. Furnivall, *op. cit.*, p. 53.

36. Burma, Crime Enquiry Committee, *Report*, p. 5.

37. Burma, *Village Administration in Burma, 1934-39*, p. 11.

38. Burma, *Report on the Administration of Burma, 1924*, p. 20.

39. Royal Commission on Agriculture in India, Volume XII, *Evidence Taken in Burma*, pp. 76, 212.

NOTES FOR CHAPTER 8

1. See above, p. 96.

2. J. Russell Andrus, *Burmese Economic Life* (Stanford, Calif., 1948), p. 40.

3. The average yearly dividend paid by the Burmah Oil Company over twenty years was 21.8 percent. Callis, *Foreign Capital in Southeast Asia* (New York, 1942), p. 89. The Burma Corporation Ltd., the leading mining company, earned an average dividend of 7 percent from 1928 to 1938. Ibid., p. 90.

4. Furnivall, op. cit., p. 187.

5. The transfer of commercial profits to all countries amounted to ten to twelve million pounds annually over the yeriod 1929-1939. Callis, op. cit., p. 93.

6. Furnivall, An Introduction to the Political Economy of Burma (Rangoon, 1938), p. 39.

7. Sir George Scott, Burma: A Handbook of Practical Information, pp. 280-281.

8. Andrus, op, cit., p. 27.

9. Furnivall, Colonial Policy and Practice, p. 51.

10. Ibid., p. 96.

11. Burma, Annual Report on Maritime Trade and Commerce (1881-2), p. 38.

12. Furnivall, op, cit., p. 97.

13. Ibid.

14. Ownership of Rice Mills by Ethnic Groups-- 1939 /Furnivall, op. cit., p. 189/: Europeans-- 27; Chinese--164; Indians--190; Burmese and other indigenous peoples--311.

15. Great Britain, Indian Statutory Commission, Volume IV, Extracts from Official Oral Evidence, p. 160.

16. Ibid. In the year 1939-1940 the long-term leasees extracted 307,997 tons of the total 400,159 tons logged in Burma. Andrus, op. cit., p. 105.

17. Scott, op. cit., pp. 238-239.

18. Andrus, op. cit., p. 116.

19. Great Britain, Indian Statutory Commission, Volume XI, Memorandum Submitted by the Government of Burma, p. 22.

20. The sale of the Burma Spinning and Weaving Company stock had raised only Rs. 1,100,000 of the authorized capital of Rs. 3,000,000 and Rs. 1,500,000 was borrowed from private sources

at interest rates of from 12 to 18 percent per annum. Great Britain, Indian Statutory Commission, Volume XI, <u>Memorandum Submitted by the Government of Burma,</u> p. 132.

21. Ibid.

22. Christian, <u>op</u>. <u>cit</u>., p. 136.

23. Callis, <u>op</u>. <u>cit</u>., p. 91.

24. The Chettyar holdings in 1939 were valued at 50 million pounds, about equaling the value of all the major British investments. Furnivall, <u>op</u>. <u>cit</u>., p. 190.

25. Furnivall, <u>op</u>. <u>cit</u>., p. 111.

26. Great Britain, Indian Statutory Commission, Volume XI, <u>Memorandum Submitted by the Government of Burma,</u> p. 20.

27. Ibid.

28. Great Britain, Indian Statutory Commission, Volume XI, <u>Memorandum Submitted by the Government of Burma</u>, p. 273.

29. Ibid., p. 133.

30. Burma Round Table Conference, London, 1931-32, <u>Proceedings,</u> Cmd. 4004 (1932), pp. 39-40.

31. Great Britain, Parliament, Joint Committee on Indian Constitutional Reform /Session 1933-34/, Volume II, <u>Records,</u> p. 198.

32. <u>Burma Gazette</u> (Part I), 1916, p. 24.

33. See pp. 163-164.

34. Burma, Financial Commissioner, <u>Report on the Working of the Co-operative Societies Act in Burma, 1925,</u> p. 13.

35. Burma, Financial Commissioner, <u>Report on the Working of the Co-operative Societies Act in Burma, 1924,</u> p. 11.

36. See chart showing the number and membership of nonagricultural cooperative societies. Appendix F.

37.   Burma Gazette, Supplement, 1924, p. 361.

38.   Great Britain, Indian Statutory Commission, Volume XI, Memorandum Submitted by the Government of Burma, p. 527.

39.   Great Britain, Report of the Committee on Financial Relations, Cmd. 724 (1920).

40   Burma Gazette, Supplement, 1920, p. 1248.

41   Burma Gazette, Supplement, 1922, p. 375.

BIBLIOGRAPHY

Official Publications

The Burma Gazette, published weekly by the
Burma government, Rangoon, contains a wide variety
of valuable information on the functioning of the
British administration. The following types of
materials were particularly useful: (1) abstracts
of the Proceedings of the Burma Legislative Council
(prior to 1923); (2) summaries of meetings of departments of the Burma government and special committees; (3) reports of special committees; (4)
extracts from The Gazette of India applicable to
Burma; (5) acts, ordinances, and notifications;
(6) special Orders outlawing athins, listing
criminal tribes, and seizing seditious publications;
(7) Instruments of Instruction issued to the
Governors; (8) special reports; e.g., "Shooting
Affray at Padinbin" in the 1928 Supplement to the
Burma Gazette. (Traces the operation of a village
Wunthanu athin and the origins of a clash between
the police and the Padinbin villagers.)

The Burma Gazette also contains considerable
material on the personnel of the administration,
education, public works, trade and commerce, publications, and legislation under consideration.

Collections of legislation applicable to Burma
include: The Gazette of India, New Delhi, weekly;
India, A Collection of Acts Passed by the Governor-
General of India in Council; India, Legislative
Department, Unrepealed General Acts (1930);
Great Britain, The Public General Acts, Annually;
Great Britain, Statutory Rules and Orders; Great
Britain, Government of India Act and Government
of Burma Act 1935, Cmd. 5181 (1935-36).

Law reports contain only a few criminal cases
which directly concern the relations between the
Burmese nationalists and the government. Some
of the civil cases illustrate the economic difficulties of the Burma's agriculturalists. The bulk
of the relevant cases after 1921 are found in the
annual Indian Law Reports (Rangoon Series). Cases
tried under the Anti-Boycott Act and appeals from
the Burma Rebellion (Trials) Ordinance give re-
vealing insights into particular incidents.

The Burma government published annual reports
on the operations of almost all of its departments.
The Report on the Administration of Burma is a
general summary of the departmental reports as
well as an overview of developments in Burma during

the year. This Report is the most useful general
source of information although stereotypes tended
to develop in presenting information, particularly
in describing political events.

The Burma Police Department's annual Report on
the Police Administration in Burma gives regular
accounts of the growth of crime and the attendant
social disintegration. There is little information
on the work of the Criminal Investigation Department, which scrutinized political activity. The
Reports describe the growth of the village athins
during the 1920s. Extracts from the reports of
the divisional police commissioners give a variety
of insights into political and social problems in
Burma. The Burma, Police Department, Report on
Criminal Justice (annual) gives statistical data
on the disposition of criminal cases.

The Burma, Crime Enquiry Committee, Report of
the Crime Enquiry Committee (Maymyo, 1923), gives
the most comprehensive picture of internal conditions in Burma at the beginning of the period of
reform. The committee's report outlines the
organization of Burmese society as related to the
problem of crime.

Burma, Resolution Reviewing the Report
on the Working of the Municipal Committees in Burma
(Except Rangoon), annual.

Burma, Resolution on the Working of the District Councils and Other Rural Local Authorities,
annual.

Burma, Riots Enquiry Committee, Interim Report
and Final Report (Rangoon, 1939) give background
material on the Indian minority problem in Burma.
The Interim Report also gives a general description
of political developments 1930-1938.

Burma, Education Department, Annual Report on
Public Instruction in Burma traces the development
of education in Burma. Burma, Education Department,
Report of the Committee Appointed to Ascertain and
Advise How the Imperial Idea May Be Inculcated and
Fostered in Schools and Colleges in Burma (Rangoon,
1917), depicts the political attitudes of the people of Burma as conceived by the administration at
the inception of the reform period.

Burma, Financial Commissioner, Report on the
Working of the Cooperative Societies in Burma,
annual.

Burma, Financial Commissioner, Report on Land
Revenue Administration, annual--for data on the

244

antitaxation campaign.

Burma, _Annual_ _Report_ on _Maritime_ _Trade_ and _Commerce_.

Burma, Information Office, _Burma_ _Handbook_ (Simla, 1942). General information including material on political parties and elections.

Burma, Government Book Depot, _Catalogue_ of _Books_ and _Maps_ in _Stock_ at _the_ _Government_ _Book_ _Depot,_ _Rangoon_.

A particularly interesting critique of local government in Burma under the British is given in the Burma (Union), _First_ _Interim_ _Report_ of _the_ _Administration_ _Reorganization_ _Committee_ (Rangoon, 1949).

India, Council of State, _Debates,_ and India, Legislative Assembly, _Debates,_ contain few references to Burma and fewer statements by the delegates from Burma.

India, Sedition Committee, _Revolutionary_ _Conspiracies_ in _India_ (New Delhi, 1919) /also appears as Cd. 9190/, treats Indian conspiracies in Burma during World War I.

India, Home Department, _India_ in _(year)_, is an annual review of political and economic conditions in India with brief sections on events in Burma.

India, _Census_ of _India_ _1931_ (New Delhi, 1933), Volume XI, "Burma"--extensive data on population and its distribution, employment, ethnic groups, languages, etc.

The most extensive sources on British policy and administration in Burma are found in the publications of British Parliament and the India Office in London.

Great Britain, Indian Statutory Commission, _Report_ of _the_ _Indian_ _Statutory_ _Commission_ (London, 1930), 17 volumes. Contains the greatest amount of detailed information on Burma, particularly on the functioning of the 1923 reforms up to 1929. The following volumes are pertinent: I, "_Survey_," general background material. II, "_Recommendations,_" includes the commission's recommendations on Burma. III, "_Reports_ of _the_ _Committees_ _Appointed_ by _the_ _Provincial_ _Legislative_ _Councils_ to _Cooperate_ with _the_ _Indian_ _Statutory_ _Commission,_" contains the report of the moderate Burma Provincial Committee on separation, responsible government, and the minorities. XI, "_Memorandum_ _Submitted_ by _the_ _Government_ of _Burma,_" detailed information on the political developments, the functioning of the administrative departments and the Legislative

245

Council, the growth of nationalism, and the beginnings of political parties. Charts show the
voting on resolutions in the Legislative Council,
government action to implement resolutions,
elections, and other relevant data illustrating
the stages of political development in Burma. XV,
"Extracts from Official Oral Evidence." XVII,
"Selections from Memoranda and Oral Evidence by
Non-Officials."

Volumes XV and XVII present a wide variety of
opinion on the operation of the Burma government.
Volume XVII contains memoranda by nationalist
organizations which relate the early history of the
nationalist movement.

Great Britain, Parliament, The Parliamentary
Debates (Official Reports) /House of Commons7. The
Debates /Commons/ contain many of the important
policy statements on India and Burma. The more
protracted debates concerning Burma appear on the
motion to include Burma as a Governor's Province
(1919), on consideration of the draft rules on the
franchise and division of functions (1922), and
on consideration of the Government of India Bill
(1935). The Secretary of State for India was subject to protracted questioning on the Burma rebellion, and his answers give some details as to
the course of events. Great Britain, Parliament,
The Parliamentary Debates (Official Reports) /House
of Lords7, have much less information of Burma.
However, the recollections of the Lords who were
formerly high in the administration in India and
Burma provide a type of fragmentary collection of
memoirs of the early reform period.

The reports of the parliamentary committees
examining proposed legislation for India and Burma
contain a variety of materials on the functioning
of the Burma government and proposals for constitutional reform. The major reports are:

Great Britain, Parliament, Joint Com-
mittee on the Government of India Bill, Report,
Proceedings, Evidence, Appendices (Sessional
Papers, 1919, Volume IX).

Great Britain, Parliament, Standing Joint
Committee on Indian Affairs, Session 1921,
Second Report of the Committee (Sessional
Papers, 1921, Volume VI).

Great Britain, Parliament, Standing Joint
Committee on Indian Affairs, Session 1922,
First Report of the Standing Joint Committee
(Sessional Papers, 1922, Volume V).

Great Britain, Parliament, Joint Committee
on Indian Constitutional Reforms, Session

1933-34, Report, Proceedings and Records, 2 volumes.
The publications of the India Office on political institutions for Burma center about the proceedings leading to the 1923 and 1935 constitutional reforms. Most of these publications were issued as parliamentary command papers (Cd. or Cmd.).

1923 Reforms

Great Britain, India Office, Report on Indian Constitutional Reforms, Cd. 9109 (1918). The Montagu-Chelmsford Report.

Great Britain, India Office, Addresses Presented in India to the Viceroy and Secretary of State for India, Cd. 9178 (1918). Contains the appeal by the Burma deputation to Calcutta, 1918.

Great Britain, India Office, Letter from the Government of India to the Secretary of State and Enclosures, Cmd. 123 (1919).

Great Britain, India Office, Proposals of the Government of India for a New Constitution for Burma, Cmd. 746 (1920).

Great Britain, India Office, Correspondence Regarding the Application to Burma of the Government of India Act 1919, Cmd. 1671, Cmd. 1672 (1922).
The three preceding documents contain the essence of the various proposals and counterproposals for 1923 Burma reforms.

Great Britain, India Office, Burma Reform Committee, Report, Record of Evidence, 6 volumes (Rangoon-London, 1922).
The report of the Whyte Committee. Views of officials on the franchise, and division of administrative functions.

There were several evaluations of the operation of the administration during the interreform period.

Great Britain, India Office, Report of the Reforms Enquiry 1924. Cmd. 2360, 2361, 2362 (1924).

Great Britain, India Office, Views of the Local Government on the Working of the Reforms, Cmd. 2362 (1924).

Great Britain, India Office, Views of the Local Government on the Working of the Reforms (1927).

1935 Reforms

Great Britain, India Office, Report of the Indian Central Committee, 1928-29, Cmd. 3451 (1929). The Indian view on separation and reform.

Great Britain, India Office, Government of India's Despatches on Proposals for Constitutional Reform Dated 20th September, 1930, Cmd. 3700 (1930).

Great Britain, India Office, Despatches from Provincial Governments in India Containing Proposals for Constitutional Reform, Cmd. 3712 (1930).

Financial Relations of India and Burma

Great Britain, India Office, Report of the Committee on Financial Relations, Cmd. 724 (1920). The Meston Committee report.

Great Britain, India Office, Views . . . on the Report of the Committee on Financial Relations, Cmd. 794 (1920).

Great Britain, India Office, Report of the Advisory Tribunal on the Financial Settlement between India and Burma, Cmd. 4902 (1935).

Great Britain, India Office, Report on the Rebellion in Burma up to May 3, 1931 and Communique Issued by the Government of Burma May 19, 1931, Cmd. 3900 (1931).

Great Britain, India Office, Trade and Immigration Relations between India and Burma after Separation from Burma, Cmd. 4985 (1934-35).

Great Britain, India Office, Delimitation of Constituencies in Burma, Cmd. 5101 (1935-36).

Great Britain, India Office, Return Showing Results of Elections in India, Cmd. 2154 (1923); Cmd. 2923 (1925-26).

Great Britain, India Office, India Office List, annual. Personnel and positions in the administration.

Royal Commissions

Great Britain, Royal Commission on the Indian Public Services, Report of the Royal Commission on the Indian Public Services, 1913-16.

Great Britain, Royal Commission on the Superior Civil Services in India, Report of the Royal Commission on the Superior Civil Services in India, 1924.

Great Britain, Royal Commission on Indian
Currency and Finance, Report of the Royal Commission on Indian Currency and Finance, 1926.
Great Britain, Royal Commission on Agriculture in India, Report of the Royal Commission
on Agriculture in India, 1928.
Great Britain, Royal Commission on Labour in
India, Report of the Royal Commission on Labour
in India, 1931.

Conferences

Indian Round Table Conference, London, 1930-31,
Proceedings, Cmd. 3778 (1931).
Indian Round Table Conference, London, 1930-31,
Proceedings of Sub-Committees (1931). Part II,
Sub-Committee IV--Burma.
Indian Round Table Conference, London, 1930-31,
Sub-Committee's Reports; Conference Resolution; and
Prime Ministers Statement, Cmd. 3772 (1931).
The major part of the discussion on Burma at
the Indian Round Table Conference revolved around
the separation issue.
Burma Round Table Conference, London 1931-
1932, Proceedings, Cmd. 4004 (1932).
Burma Round Table Conference, London, 1931-
1932, Proceedings of the Committee of the Whole
Conference (1932).
The Burma Round Table Conference proceedings
include a wide range of nationalist opinion since
the antiseparationists participated. The history
of the GCBA is reviewed by the Burmese nationalists.
These reports contain detailed consideration of
political institutions and the attitudes of the
Burmese, the minorities, and British on the projected reforms.

Archival Materials

Reports, despatches, and telegrams from the
American Consul in Rangoon up to 1924 were examined
in the United States National Archives. Later
materials from the same source are found in the
collections of the Department of State. Of principal interest are the monthly reports on "Politics-
Economic Conditions." These reports cover agriculture, economic conditions, legislation, the
police, social organization, and current political

developments. Reports of nationalist activities, particularly of meetings, not available from other official sources are found in some of the consular reports. The reports on the rebellion of 1930-1931 and the summary of U Saw's The Burma Situation introduce new points of view on the character of the uprising. The "History of the Origins, Growth and Organization of the Burma Legislative Council," prepared by the American Consul, is a convenient summary of institutional developments. For a more detailed discussion of the available materials see, Purnendu Basu, Materials in the National Archives Relating to India (U.S. National Archives, Reference Information Circular 38, 1949). Only scattered references to Burma are found in the reports from the United States missions in New Delhi and London.

Memoirs and Biographies

Note: Asterisks indicate works which were consulted only during revision stage of this book.

*Ba, U, My Burma: The Autobiography of a President. New York: Taplinger Publishing Co., 1958. p. 210.
*Ba, Maw, U, Breakthrough in Burma: Memoirs of a Revolution, 1929-1939. New Haven, Conn.: New Haven, Conn.: Yale University Press, 1968. pp. xxiii, 460.
Butler, Sir Spencer Harcourt, Collection of Speeches. Rangoon: Government Press, 1927. pp. iv, 237.
Cadogan, Edward Cecil George, The India We Saw. London: J. Murray, 1933. pp. vii, 310. By a member of the Indian Statutory Commission.
Collis, Maurice Stewart, Trials in Burma. London: Faber & Faber, 1938. pp. x, 224. By a British magistrate in Burma. The functioning of the legal system and the origins of the 1932 rebellion.
Mi Mi Khaing, Burmese Family. London: Longmans, 1946. p. 138.
Montagu, Sir Edwin S., An Indian Dairy. Edited by Venetia Montagu. London: W. Heinemann, 1930. p. 410. The Montagu mission to India. Some insights into the decision-making process. Little information on Burma.
White, Herbert Thirkell, A Civil Servant in Burma. London: Edward Arnold, 1913. pp. xi, 314.

SECONDARY WORKS

Books

The following first eight books are of special
significance since they are written by British
officials who had first-hand experience with policy
or administration in Burma.

Amery, Leopold S., The Forward View. London: G.
    Bles, 1935. p. 464
Butler, Sir Spenser Harcourt, India Insistent. Lon-
    don: W. Heinemann, Ltd., 1931. pp. xviii,
    117.
Craddock, Sir Reginald Henry, The Dilemma in India.
    London: Constable & Co., Ltd., 1930. pp.
    xviii, 378.
Crosthwaite, Sir Charles, The Pacification of
    Burma. London: E. Arnold, 1912. pp. xii,
    355.
Furnivall, John Sydenham, An Introduction to the
    Political Economy of Burma. Rangoon: Burma
    Book Club, 1938. 2d rev. ed., edited by J.
    Russell Andrus. p. 255.
_____, Colonial Policy and Practice, A Comparative
    Study of Burma and Netherlands India. Cam-
    bridge: At the University Press, 1948. pp.
    xii, 568. Furnivall is the leading authority
    on the effects of British rule in Burma. This
    book contains summaries of official publica-
    tions not usually available.
Leach, F. Burton, The Future of Burma. Rangoon:
    British Burma Press, 1936. p. 136.
Pole, David Graham, India in Transition. London
    Hogarth Press, 1932. p. 395.

Andrew, E. J. L., Indian Labour in Rangoon. London:
    Oxford University Press, 1933. pp. xxxiii,
    300. Contains the Report of the Rangoon Riots
    Enquiry Committee, 1930.
Andrus, James Russell, Burmese Economic Life.
    Stanford, Calif.: Stanford University Press,
    1948. pp. xxii, 362.
_____, Rural Reconstruction in Burma. Oxford
    University Press, 1936. pp. xx, 145.
Appadorai, Angadipuram, Dyarchy in Practice. Lon-
    don: Longmans, Green & Co., Ltd., 1937.
    pp. xiv, 431.
Bannerjee, Anil Chandra, Annexation of Burma.
    Calcutta: A. Mukherjee & Bros., 1944. p. 388.

251

Baxter, James, Report on Indian Immigration. Rangoon: Superintendent, Goverment Printing, 1941. p. 199. A semiofficial survey of the Indian minority problem.

Blunt, Sir Edward, The I.C.S.; The Indian Civil Service. London: Faber and Faber, Ltd., 1937. pp. xii, 291.

Bose, Subhas Chandra, The Indian Struggle, 1920-1934. London: Wishart and Co., Ltd., 1935. p. 353.

*Cady, John F., A History of Modern Burma. Ithaca, New York: Cornell University Press, 1958. pp. xiv, 682.

Cady, John F., Patricia G. Barnett, and Shirley Jenkins, The Development of Self Rule and Independence in Burma, Malaya and the Philippines. New York: Institute of Pacific Relations, 1948. p. 104.

Callis, Helmut G., Foreign Capital in Southeast Asia. New York: Institute of Pacific Relations, 1942. pp. iv, 120.

The Cambridge History of India, Volumes 5, 6. New York: MacMillan Co., 1929. pp. 660, 683.

Christian, John L., Burma and the Japanese Invader. Bombay: Thacker & Co., 1945. pp. xii, 418.

Cumming, Sir John Ghest, ed., Political India 1832-1932. London: Oxford University Press, H. Mildord, 1932. pp. viii, 324.

Dautremer, Joseph, Burma under British Rule. London: Fisher Unwin, 1913. pp. xxxiv, 390.

Desai, Walter Sadgun, History of the British Residency in Burma 1828-40. Rangoon: The University of Rangoon, 1939. pp. xiv, 491.

Devas, C. S., Rebirth of Burma. Madras: Associated Printers, 1947. pp. xxiii, 268.

*Donnison, F. S. V., Administration in Burma; A Study of Development during the British Connection. London: Royal Institute of International Affairs, 1953. p. 119.

Edmunds, Paul, Peacocks and Pagodas. London: Routledge, 1924. pp. xii, 282. A general description of Burma with comments on the political capacities of its people in the early 1920s.

Emerson, Rupert, Lennox A. Mills, and Virginia Thompson, Government and Nationalism in Southeast Asia. New York: Institute of Pacific Relations, 1942. pp. xiii, 242.

*Hall, Daniel George Edward, Burma. London: Hutchinson's University Library, 1950. p. 184.

Harvey, Godfrey Eric, British Rule in Burma 1824-1942. London: Faber & Faber, 1946. p. 100.

Ireland, Alleyne, The Province of Burma. 2 volumes.

New York: Houghton Mifflin, 1907. A compen-
dium of information on British rule in Burma
in the nineteenth century taken from official
sources.

Jacoby, Erich H., Agrarian Unrest in Southeast
Asia. New York: Columbia University Press,
1949. pp. xix, 287.

Laymen's Foreign Mission Inquiry, Fact Finders
Reports, "India--Burma," Volume 4, Part II.
New York: Institute of Social Research,
1933. Contains information on the relation of
Buddhism to nationalism.

*Sarkisyanz, Emanuel, Buddhist Backgrounds of the
Burma Revolution. The Hague: M. Nijhoff,
1965. pp. xxix, 248.

Scott, Sir James George, Burma: A Handbook of
Practical Information. London: Alexander
Moring, Ltd., 1906. pp. x, 520.

Sen, Nirmal Chandra, A Peep into Burma Politics
1917-1937. Allhabad: Kitabistan Press,
1945. p. 85. Unreliable and incomplete but
it does give alignments of political groups
not available elsewhere.

Singh, Ganga, Burma Parliamentary Companion.
Rangoon: British Burma Press (Rangoon
Gazette, Ltd.), 1940. pp. iv, 689.

*Smith, Donald E., Religion and Politics in Burma.
Princeton: Princeton University Press, 1965.
p. 350.

Smith, William Roy, Nationalism and Reform in India.
New Haven: Yale University Press, 1938. p.
485.

Thompson, Edward J. and G. T. Garatt, Rise and Ful-
fillment of British Rule in India. London:
MacMillan and Co., 1934. p. 690.

*Thompson, John Seaburg, "Marxism in Burma," in
Frank N. Trager (ed.), Marxism in Southeast
Asia, A Study of Four Countries. Stanford:
Stanford University Press, 1959. pp. 14-57.

*Trager, Frank N., Burma: From Kingdom to Republic;
A Historical and Political Analysis. New
York: Praeger, 1966. pp. xiii, 455.

*Von der Mehden, Fred R., Religion and Nationalism
in Southeast Asia: Burma, Indonesia and the
Philippines. Madison: University of Wisconsin
Press, 1968. p. 253.

Wales, Horace Geoffrey Quaritch, Years of Blindness. New York: Crowell, 1943. p. 332. The
interaction of Western institutions and
Asian societies.

Warren, C. V., Burmese Interlude. London: Skef-
fington, 1937. p. 288.

Wint, Guy, The British in Asia. London: Faber &

Faber, 1947. p. 224.

The following important books covering the
period were not available to this author.

Collis, Maurice Stewart, Into Hidden Burma; An
    Autobiography. London: Faber & Faber, 1953.
    p. 268.
Maung Maung, Pye, Burma in the Crucible. Rangoon:
    Khittaya Publishing House, 1952. pp. vi, 212.
Tinker, Hugh, The Foundations of Local Self-Govern-
    ment in India, Pakistan and Burma. London:
    University of London, Athlone Press, 1954.
    pp. xxiv, 376.

Periodicals

The following first thirteen articles are by
former officials and usually reflect their personal
experiences.

Bigg-Wither, F., "Cleaning Up Burma's Murder Zone,"
    Contemporary Review, Volume 56 (1939), pp.
    715-722.
Butler, Spencer Harcourt, "Burma and Its Problems,"
    Foreign Affairs, Volume 10 (1932), pp. 647-
    658
Collis, Maurice, "The Burma Scene," Geographical
    Magazine, Volume 7 (1938), pp. 405-422.
Craddock, Reginald, "The Simon Report and After,"
    Nineteenth Century, Volume 108 (1930), pp.
    160-168.
Fuller, A. G., "Disorders in Burma," Journal of the
    Royal United Service Institution, Volume 76
    (1931), pp. 530-533.
Furnivall, John S., "The Fashioning of Leviathan,"
    Journal of the Burma Research Society, Volume
    29 (1938), pp. 1-137.
_____, "Administration in Burma," Asiatic Review,
    Volume 31 (1925), pp. 653-668.
Innes, Sir Charles, "Constitutional Future of
    Burma," Great Britain and the East, Volume 43
    (1934), p. 66.
_____, "Burma and His Place in the Empire,"
    United Empire, Volume 25, New Series (1934),
    pp. 211-220.
_____, "The Separation of Burma," Asiatic Review,
    Volume 30 (1934), pp. 193-214.
Leach, Burton, "Autonomy on Trial in Burma,"
    Asiatic Review, Volume 35 (1939), pp. 631-654.
Lewis, Hilary, "Rebellion," Army Quarterly, Volume

25 (1932), pp. 312-320.
Page, Sir Arthur, "Burma in Transition," Asiatic
    Review, Volume 34 (1938), pp. 225-243.

Anup, Singh, "The Rebel Premier of Burma," Asia,
    Volume 42 (1942), pp. 17-18.
Appleton, G., "The Burmese Viewpoint," Journal of
    the Royal Society of the Arts, Volume 96,
    No. 4771 (1928), pp. 439-455.
Brown, R. G., "Burma," Asiatic Review, Volume 22
    (1936), pp. 570-572.
Christian, John, "Burma between Two Wars," Asia,
    Volume 41 (1941), pp. 446-449.
_____, "Burma Divorces India," Current History,
    Volume 46 (1937), pp. 82-86.
Craw, Henry, "Burma," Asiatic Review, Volume 38
    . (1943), pp. 259-266.
Enriques, Colin M. D., "Burma's Relation to India,"
    English Review, Volume 47 (1928), pp. 561-565.
_____, "Rebel Activities," National Review, Volume
    100 (1933), pp. 90-92.
Hobbs, Cecil, "Nationalism in British Colonial
    Burma," Far Eastern Quarterly, Volume 6
    (1946), pp. 113-121.
_____, "Curiosities of the Burma Rebellion,"
    Illustrated London News, Volume 181 (1932),
    p. 350.
Nolan, J. J., "Burma, An Unofficial View," Asiatic
    Review, Volume 24 (1928), pp. 225-251.
Stephenson, Sir Hugh, "Some Problems of a Separated
    Burma," Journal of the Royal Central Asian
    Society, Volume 25 (1938), pp. 400-415.
Strickland, C. F., "Burma's Demand for Home
    Rule," Current History, Volume 35 (1932),
    pp. 855-858.
Sutton, Walter, Jr., "U Aung San of Burma," South
    Atlantic Quarterly, Volume 47 (1948), pp. 1-16.
Swithinbank, Bernard W., "Responsible Government,"
    Asiatic Review, Volume 39 (1943), pp. 153-160.

Newspapers

Daily News (London).
Times (London). See especially "Burma Supplement,"
    April 20, 1937, p. 40.

The following Indian nationalist newspapers
were examined for the periods of political tension
in Burma. Manifestos, letters, and telegrams by
Burmese nationalists are sometimes published.

Forward (Calcutta).
Indian Daily News (Calcutta).
Liberty (Calcutta).

INDEX

19-20, 188. See also nationalist movement
Burmese peasant, 18, 38, 114, 175; discontent of,
    39, 57, 118-119, 177, 180. See also Buddhism,
    in peasant's life
Burmese (people), and the franchise, 136-140, 191,
    193-194, 234 n. 4; literacy of, 2; social
    cohesiveness of, 12, 180; as soldiers, 132,
    133-134, 194
business: Burmese government aid to, 169-172;
    Burmese lack of experience in, 156, 161-164,
    169, 171-172

capitation tax, 45, 46, 51, 57, 136, 140
Chelmsford, Lord, 25
Chettyars. See Indians
Chinese (minority), 120-121
Chins, 116
Chit Hlaing, U, 27, 38, 63, 64, 67, 92, 219 n. 46,
    222 n. 77
Circle Boards, 35, 145-148, 194
civil servants: Burmese, 15, 100-102, 104-105,
    106, 111-112, 188, 189-190; Indian, 108-109
Committee on the Imperial Idea, 22
communal representation, 123-124, 126, 127, 128
constitution, Burmese, 1935, 92, 95, 97-98, 186-187
cooperative societies or enterprises, 170-172
cottage or handicraft industries, 162-164, 168-169,
    170, 172, 196
Council of Ministers, under Government of Burma
    Act, 1935, 96
Craddock, Governor, 25, 26, 32-33, 72-73, 75,
    132, 217 n. 22
"Craddock Scheme," 72-73
Crime Enquiry Committee, 1923, 11, 38
crime rate, 11, 151, 179
Criminal Tribes Act, 142

District Councils, 145, 147-148, 194
Dobama, or "We Burmans" society, 56, 65, 120
Dobama Asi Ayon (We Burmans Association), 65-66
dyarchy, 62, 80-81, 83, 84, 183, 185-186

education, Burmese, higher, 107
education, ministry of, 79, 81, 187
elections, to legislature, 1922, 35-36, 138; 1925,
    49-50, 138; 1928, 53; 1932, 62-63; 1936, 67-68

forestry: department of, 9; ministry of, 79, 81,
    187

General Council of Burmese Associations (GCBA),
    32, 33, 34-35, 38, 41, 47-48, 49, 61-62, 167
General Council of Sangha Sametygis (pongyi asso-

ciations coalition), 36-37, 39, 40-41, 55
de Glanville, Sir Oscar, 53-54, 64
Golden Valley Party, 49-50
Government of Burma Act, 1935, 95, 126, 131, 192
Government of India Act, 1919, 27
Governor-General in New Delhi, 14, 82
Governor of Burma, under Government of Burma
    Act, 1935, 92-96, 98, 186-187, 191-192;
    role and power of, 82, 92, 140-142, 154
Gyi, Sir Joseph Maung, 58, 63, 64

hartal. See boycott
Hlaing-Pu-Gyaw (HPG) Party, 35-36, 41, 48, 49
home rule, 28-29, 31, 33, 47. See also independ-
    ence, Burmese
Home Rule Party, 49, 50, 62
Houghton, Bernard, 75
Hundred Committee, 52

import commodities, monopoly of, 162, 164, 172
independence, Burmese, 1, 87, 93-95, 102-103. See
    also home rule
Independent Party, 49-50, 53, 63, 67
Indian, laborers, 5, 39, 117-118, 191; administra-
    tive system, 7, 13, 80, 123-124; civil
    servants, 108-109; Civil Service, 15, 104-105,
    109-110; immigrants, 13, 117-118, 130-131;
    as minority, 14, 51, 117, 118, 126-127; money-
    lenders (Chettyar), 20, 43, 118, 158, 164,
    165-166, 190-191, 238 n. 24; revolutionary
    movement, 22
Indian Legislative Council, 62
Indian National Congress, 62
Indian Round Table Conference, 61, 89
individual rights, 140, 143-144
industrialization, 162-163
Innes, Sir Charles, 58, 59

Kachins, 116
Karens, 87, 114-115, 116-117, 126-127, 132, 190
Kin, U, 21
Komin Kochin (One's Own King, One's Own Kind),
    66, 67
Kyaw Din, 64

Legislative Council (1897), 9, 10, 70-71, 82,
    213-214 n. 10
Legislative Council, 35-36, 46, 49, 50-51, 53-54,
    64, 81, 82, 123, 124, 126-127, 128
legislature, under Government of Burma Act, 1935,
    97-98
literacy, 2
local government, 7-8, 11-12, ·110, 145, 195; self-

261

rule of, 144, 148, 151
luthat (murder associations), 44

Marxist ideology, 65
Maung Chit Pe, 76
Maung Gyee, U, 36
Maung Po Pe, 34
May Oung, U, 21, 50, 217 n. 19
Mehta, P. J., 75
Meston Committee, 76, 173
mining, 162
monastery schools, 2
Mons. See Talaings
Montagu, Edwin, Secretary of State for India, 24,
    71, 75, 76, 226 n. 3, n. 4
Montagu-Chelmsford Report, 25-26, 71-72, 131
Montagu Declaration, 25, 75, 77, 185
Municipal Councils, 10, 11, 149-151, 195, 214 n. 14
Myint, U, 218 n. 38

nationalist movement, 17-18, 19-20, 23, 24, 28, 30,
    33, 55, 125-126, 155, 166, 183-184, 214 n, 215
    n. 1, n. 2, 232 n. 23; and agrarian discontent,
    21, 155, 180; at the village level, 33, 57,
    60, 181
National Parliamentary Organization, 53. See also
    People's Party
national schools, 30
Nationalist Party, 35-36, 37, 38, 49, 50, 53, 83
Ngabwinsaing (Five Groups Alliance) Party, 67
1931-1932 rebellion, 51-52, 54, 167
noncooperation movement, 27, 29-20, 32, 38, 41-42,
    186
nonindigenous minorities, 14, 113, 117, 121-122,
    125, 187, 190, 191-192
Nu, Thakin, 66

oil fields, 161
Older Party, 26, 31
Ottama, U, 19, 31-32, 33-34, 38, 40, 41, 47-48, 50,
    51, 223 n. 2

pagoda footwear controversy, 23-24
Paungde Conference, 45, 47, 223 n. 2
peasants, conditions of, 13-14, 20-21, 38, 57, 60,
    158
People's Party, 50, 53, 63, 67; merged with National
    Parliamentary Organization, 53
police, 37, 111
political apathy, 138-139, 144-145
political reforms, 2-3, 10, 116, 157, 167, 182,
    183, 197
pongyis, 39, 40, 41, 49, 58-59, 181-182

violence, in nationalist movement, 24, 44, 55-56, 58-59

Westernization and acculturation, 4-5, 11, 18, 45, 57, 58, 60, 177-178, 180-181, 197
Whyte Committee. See Burma Reforms Committee
Whyte, Frederick, 31, 77
Wizaya, U, 54
wunthanu athins (nationalist associations), 33, 38, 41, 222 n. 73

Young Burman Group, 76
Younger Party, 26, 31, 217 n. 22
Young Men's Buddhist Association (YMBA), 21-22, 23, 25, 29, 31

PREVIOUSLY PUBLISHED

(No. 1) <u>Bibliography of English Language Sources on Human Ecology, Eastern Malaysia and Brunei</u>. Compiled by Conrad P. Cotter with the assistance of Shiro Saito. September 1965. Two parts. Out of print.

(No. 2) <u>Economic Factors in Southeast Asian Social Change</u>. May 1968. Robert Van Niel, editor. Out of print.

No. 3 <u>East Asian Occasional Papers (1)</u>. Harry J. Lamley, editor. May 1969

No. 4 <u>East Asian Occasional Papers (2)</u>. Harry J. Lamley, editor. July 1970.

No. 5 <u>A Survey of Historical Source Materials in Java and Manila</u>. Robert Van Niel. February 1971.

(No. 6) <u>Educational Theory in the People's Republic of China: The Report of Ch'ien Chung-Jui</u>. Translation by John N. Hawkins. May 1971. Out of print.

No. 7 <u>Hai Jui Dismissed from Office</u>. Wu Han. Translation by C. C. Huang. June 1972.

No. 8 <u>Aspects of Vietnamese History</u>. Edited by Walter F. Vella. March 1973.

No. 9 <u>Southeast Asian Literatures in Translation: A Preliminary Bibliography</u>. Philip N. Jenner. March 1973.

No. 10 <u>Textiles of the Indonesian Archipelago</u>. Garrett and Bronwen Solyom. October 1973.